Better Homes and Gardens ®

Favorite RECIPES FROM COUNTRY INNS
& BED-AND-BREAKFASTS

Our seal assures you that every recipe in *Favorite Recipes from Country Inns and Bed-and-Breakfasts* has been tested in the Better Homes and Gardens® Test Kitchen. This means that each recipe is practical and reliable, and meets our high standards of taste appeal. We guarantee your satisfaction with this book for as long as you own it.

WE CARE!

All of us at Better Homes and Gardens® Books are dedicated to providing you with the information and ideas you need to create tasty foods. We welcome your comments or suggestions. Write us at: Better Homes and Gardens® Books, Cookbook Editorial Department, LS-348, 1716 Locust Street, Des Moines, IA 50336

On the front cover: Poached Pears with Grand Marnier Sauce (see recipe, page 107)

I stayed at my first country inns and bed-and-breakfasts a few years ago while on a bike trip in Vermont. I immediately fell in love with the country inn experience—good food, good company, and a comfortable place to lay my head. I was able to enjoy amenities such as a hearty breakfast served family style in the inn's kitchen, cookies and lemonade after a long day of biking, and a relaxing sing-along in the evening. ◆ When I set out to write this cookbook, I hoped I could share a bit of this country inn experience with you. So, with the gracious help of the innkeepers, I've collected in this book wonderful recipes exemplifying the fine food that America's inns offer. You'll also become acquainted with the charming personality of each inn. And, you'll discover five menus that you can make in your own home. ◆ Though the only way to totally experience a country inn is to visit one yourself, I hope this book will bring their essence into your home.

Mary Jo Plutt

CHAPTERS

MENUS

*H*ere are five complete meals from
selected country inns and bed-and-breakfasts you can easily make at home.

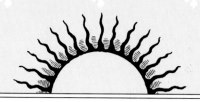

Rise'n'Shine

Mmmm—the tastes of

hot-from-the-oven muffins, fresh fruit-juice drinks, and cheesy egg entrées . . .

Now you can savor those same marvelous flavors that

delighted you while you were vacationing at your favorite country inn

or bed-and-breakfast. From their homes to yours, selected innkeepers

share their best and most-requested breakfast and brunch recipes.

A comfortable place to sleep and something good to eat go hand in hand at the **Park Row Bed & Breakfast** in St. Peter, Minnesota. Innkeeper Ann L. Burckhardt recently adapted an 1878 Victorian house into a bed-and-breakfast featuring three charming guest rooms. Ann, a food writer for 19 years, knows the importance of serving a tantalizing breakfast. She creates or adapts many of her recipes to suit the tastes of her guests. To those who don't drink coffee, Ann offers a bottom-less glass of juice. These "Fuzzy" Fruit Juice Cocktails are the result of combining a variety of fruit flavors. Ann says it has become a favorite with her guests.

"FUZZY" FRUIT JUICE COCKTAILS

2 cups *ice* water
⅓ cup frozen peach daiquiri mix, thawed*
⅓ cup frozen orange juice concentrate, thawed
Fresh mint (optional)

In a blender container or food processor bowl place the ice water, peach daiquiri mix, and orange juice concentrate. Cover and blend or process till foamy. ♦ To serve, pour the juice cocktail into 5 chilled stemmed glasses. If desired, garnish with mint. Makes 5 (5½-ounce) servings.
♦ *You may substitute ⅓ cup frozen *peach juice blend concentrate,* thawed, and 2 teaspoons *lime juice* for the ⅓ cup frozen peach daiquiri mix.

"Our aim is to pamper," say Jim and Rosemary Wessely, innkeepers at **The Andrew King House,** part of an 1827 plantation just 20 minutes from St. Louis. And pamper they do. Jim and Rosemary greet their arriving guests with complimentary wine and cheese. In the evening, dreams are always a bit sweeter after guests discover a plate of homemade chocolates or cookies in their rooms. And in the morning, Jim and Rosemary treat their guests to a three-course gourmet breakfast served in the formal dining room. Rosemary uses her best china, crystal, sterling, and lace tablecloths to create an event that is not only special, but also memorable.

SWIRLED MELON SOUP

**1 2½- to 3-pound cantaloupe, seeded, peeled, and
coarsely chopped (3 cups)
2 tablespoons orange juice
4 teaspoons sugar
1 2½- to 3-pound honeydew melon, seeded, peeled, and
coarsely chopped (3 cups)
2 tablespoons dry sherry
Edible marigolds (optional) ♦ Fresh mint (optional)**

In a blender container or food processor bowl place chopped cantaloupe, *1 tablespoon* of the orange juice, and *2 teaspoons* of the sugar. Cover and blend or process till smooth. Transfer mixture to a covered airtight container. ♦ Wash blender container or food processor bowl. ♦ In the blender container or food processor bowl place chopped honeydew melon, the remaining orange juice, and the remaining sugar. Cover and blend or process till smooth. Transfer honeydew mixture to another covered airtight container. ♦ Chill the cantaloupe and the honeydew mixtures for 4 to 12 hours. ♦ To serve, stir *1 tablespoon* of the dry sherry into *each* of the melon mixtures. At the same time, pour ⅓ *cup* cantaloupe mixture and ⅓ *cup* honeydew melon mixture into *each* soup bowl. Use a narrow metal spatula or spoon to gently swirl the two mixtures. If desired, garnish with marigolds and mint. Makes 6 (⅔-cup) servings.

Cape May, New Jersey, is a town committed to preserving its Victorian past. In keeping with the town's theme, Nan and Tom Hawkins, innkeepers of the **Barnard-Good House,** are preserving the Victorian tradition of the communal breakfast, where guests share good food and good conversation. They regularly serve these imaginative four-course morning meals, which begin with one of Tom's fresh juice combinations. It might be strawberry with orange, carrot with apple, or even pineapple with cranberry and lime juice. Next is one of Nan's famous fruit soups. That is followed by a creative entrée such as wild rice 'n' walnut pancakes or crab hash with poached eggs. Finally, the grand ending to each feast is dessert. As one guest commented, "Barnard-Good House is a great place to stay. On a scale of 1 to 10, it's a 15!"

APPLE SOUP

5 medium Granny Smith *or* Golden Delicious apples, cored and halved (about 1¾ pounds total)
1 cup water
1 cup apple juice
⅓ cup sugar
4 inches stick cinnamon
1½ cups light cream *or* half-and-half
1 medium Granny Smith *or* Golden Delicious apple, cored and coarsely chopped (about 1 cup)
⅔ cup orange juice
¼ cup Grand Marnier
1 tablespoon lemon juice

In a heavy large saucepan combine the apple halves, water, apple juice, sugar, and stick cinnamon. Bring to boiling, then reduce heat. Cover and simmer over medium heat about 10 minutes or till apples are very tender. Remove from heat and cool to room temperature. ♦ Remove apples from cooking liquid and scrape apple pulp from peels. Discard peels and stick cinnamon. ♦ In a blender container or food processor bowl place *half* of the apple pulp and *half* of the cooking liquid. Cover and blend or process till smooth. Transfer apple mixture to a large mixing bowl. Repeat with remaining apple pulp and cooking liquid. Then stir in light cream, chopped apple, orange juice, Grand Marnier, and lemon juice. ♦ Cover surface of soup with plastic wrap, and chill for 6 to 24 hours. Makes 8 (¾-cup) servings.

Breakfast has become a feature at **The Inn at Union Pier** in Michigan. After a restful sleep in one of the inn's 15 attractive rooms, which are furnished with Swedish ceramic fireplaces (called *kakelugns*), guests begin their day with a hearty multiple-course breakfast. On Sunday mornings, that breakfast takes the form of a special Union Pier buffet. This Blintz Soufflé with Blueberry Sauce is a popular item on the buffet. It has the same wonderful taste as traditional blintzes, yet it's much easier to make and serve.

BLINTZ SOUFFLÉ

1 cup small-curd cottage cheese
1 3-ounce package cream cheese, softened
1 egg yolk
1½ teaspoons sugar
½ teaspoon vanilla
¾ cup dairy sour cream
¼ cup butter *or* margarine, softened
¾ teaspoon finely shredded orange peel
¼ cup orange juice
3 eggs
½ cup all-purpose flour
3 tablespoons sugar
1 teaspoon baking powder
1 recipe Blueberry Sauce

Grease an 8x8x2-inch baking dish; set aside. ♦ For filling, in a small bowl beat cottage cheese, cream cheese, egg yolk, 1½ teaspoons sugar, and vanilla with an electric mixer about 3 minutes or till nearly smooth. Set filling aside. ♦ For batter, in a medium bowl beat sour cream, butter, orange peel, orange juice, and whole eggs on low speed till smooth. Add flour, 3 tablespoons sugar, and baking powder. Beat about 2 minutes or till nearly smooth. ♦ To assemble, spread *half* of the batter into the prepared baking dish. Dollop cheese filling in small spoonfuls on top. Carefully spread remaining batter on top. ♦ Bake in a 350° oven about 40 minutes or till puffy and golden. Immediately serve with Blueberry Sauce. Makes 6 servings.

♦ **Blueberry Sauce:** In a saucepan stir together ½ cup *sugar*, 4 teaspoons *cornstarch*, ⅛ teaspoon ground *cinnamon,* and ⅛ teaspoon ground *nutmeg.* Gradually stir in ⅔ cup *water.* Cook and stir till thickened and bubbly. Then cook and stir 2 minutes more. Stir in 1⅓ cups fresh *or* frozen *blueberries* and 2 tablespoons *lemon juice.* Makes about 1⅓ cups.

Southern hospitality is at its best at **Hachland Hill** in Tennessee. As guests arrive, innkeeper Phila Hach cheerfully shows them to their rooms in the main house or to a 1790 cedar-log cabin. Much of this inn's charm comes from the 18th-century American-made antiques, feather pillows, hand-made quilts, and white starched bed linens that furnish and decorate the guest rooms and cabins. To top off a stay at Hachland Hill, Phila serves an old-time, Southern plantation, buffet breakfast. Tennessee country ham, Hachland Hill's Egg Soufflé, hash brown potatoes, cheese grits, and sugar biscuits with homemade jelly are only a few of the choices at this grand breakfast.

HACHLAND HILL'S EGG SOUFFLÉ

¼ **cup margarine** *or* **butter**
¼ **cup all-purpose flour**
½ **teaspoon curry powder**
¼ **teaspoon salt**
¼ **teaspoon pepper**
3 **cups light cream, half-and-half,** *or* **milk**
½ **teaspoon Worcestershire sauce**
8 **hard-cooked eggs, chopped**
12 **ounces sliced bacon, crisp-cooked, drained, and crumbled**

For the curry sauce, in a large saucepan melt margarine or butter. Stir in flour, curry powder, salt, and pepper. Add cream, half-and-half, or milk all at once. Cook and stir over medium heat till thickened and bubbly. Remove from heat, then stir in Worcestershire sauce. ♦ In a 2-quart casserole layer *half* of the chopped hard-cooked eggs, *half* of the curry sauce, and *half* of the bacon. Repeat layering with remaining hard-cooked eggs, curry sauce, and bacon. ♦ Bake, uncovered, in a 350° oven for 20 to 25 minutes or till heated through. Let stand for 10 minutes before serving. Makes 6 to 8 servings.

Puffy Crab Omelet
(see recipe, page 14)

Located in a storybook wilderness setting is a beautiful lodge called **Glacier Bay Country Inn**. The property originally was part of the untouched wetlands of Alaska, and the inn-keepers, Al and Annie Unrein, had to work hard to clear the land to build the remote inn. As one of the many amenities offered at Glacier Bay Country Inn, Al and Annie arrange tours for their guests. Guests can choose activities such as viewing humpback whales, salmon and halibut fishing, hiking by glaciers, kayaking to Pleasant Island, bird watching, or bicycling on the quiet country roads. Whether a guest chooses one of these adventures or just quiet time at the inn, Al's and Annie's warm and personal attention makes a stay at Glacier Bay Country Inn unforgettable.

PUFFY CRAB OMELET
(Pictured on page 13)

¾ **cup butter *or* margarine**
¾ **cup all-purpose flour**
¼ **teaspoon salt**
¼ **teaspoon ground nutmeg**
1½ **cups milk**
6 **eggs**
2 **tablespoons butter *or* margarine**
2 **tablespoons all-purpose flour**
Dash salt
Dash ground red pepper
1⅓ **cups whipping cream**
2 **tablespoons dry sherry**
2 **cups coarsely flaked, cooked Dungeness crabmeat**
***or* other cooked crabmeat**
Whipping cream
Lemon twists (optional)
Fresh dill (optional) ♦ Edible violas (optional)
Sliced King crab legs
***or* other cooked crabmeat, chopped (optional)**

Butter a 15x10x1-inch baking pan. Line the pan with waxed paper, then butter and flour the paper. Set pan aside. ♦ For omelet, in a heavy medium saucepan melt ¾ cup butter or margarine. Stir in the ¾ cup flour, ¼ teaspoon salt, and nutmeg. Add milk. Cook and stir over medium-high heat till mixture follows the spoon around the saucepan. Remove from heat and cool for 5 minutes.

Add eggs, one at a time, beating with a wire whisk till combined. Spread egg mixture in the prepared baking pan. Bake in a 400° oven for 20 to 25 minutes or till the omelet is puffy and golden. ◆ Meanwhile, for filling, in a heavy saucepan melt the 2 tablespoons butter or margarine. Stir in the 2 tablespoons flour, dash salt, and red pepper. Add the 1⅓ cups whipping cream all at once. Cook and stir till thickened and bubbly. Add sherry, then cook and stir for 1 minute more. Stir in the 2 cups crabmeat. Cook just till heated through. Set filling aside. ◆ Line a flat surface with a large sheet of waxed paper. When the omelet is done, *immediately* loosen it from the pan and invert the omelet onto the sheet of waxed paper (omelet will fall out). Peel off paper from the bottom of the omelet. Spread omelet with *three-fourths* of the filling. Roll up omelet *without* the waxed paper, jelly-roll style, starting from one of the short sides. ◆ Transfer the omelet roll to a serving platter, seam side down. ◆ Stir *1 to 2 tablespoons* of the additional whipping cream into the remaining filling, then spoon mixture on top of the omelet roll. If desired, garnish with lemon twists, dill, violas, and additional sliced or chopped crab. Makes 8 servings.

◆ **Note:** To make ahead, bake omelet up to 1 hour before serving. Leave omelet in pan. To serve, reheat omelet in a 400° oven for 5 to 8 minutes. Remove omelet from pan, fill, roll, and garnish as above.

Their ability to create unique, delicious dishes has gained innkeepers Laurie Anderson and David Campiche the reputation for serving the best breakfast in the state. At **The Shelburne Country Inn** in Seaview, Washington, Laurie and David rely on local products such as Pacific salmon, Long Beach cranberries, fiddlehead ferns, and many varieties of wild edible mushrooms and berries to add creativity and freshness to their menus. Typical morning fare at this almost-100-year-old inn might be County Salmon Pie accompanied by Laurie's homemade pastries, one of the Shelburne's many different potato recipes, fresh fruit, and freshly brewed coffee.

COUNTRY SALMON PIE

1¼ **cups all-purpose flour**
⅓ **cup grated Parmesan cheese**
½ **cup** *cold* **unsalted butter**
¼ **cup** *cold* **water**
12 **ounces fully cooked smoked salmon**
1 **large onion, chopped (1 cup)**
1 **clove garlic, minced**
3 **tablespoons unsalted butter**
5 **beaten eggs**
2¼ **cups dairy sour cream**
¼ **cup all-purpose flour**
1½ **cups shredded Gruyère** *or* **Swiss cheese (6 ounces)**
1 **tablespoon snipped fresh dill** *or* 1 **teaspoon dried dillweed**

For crust, in a bowl combine 1¼ cups flour and Parmesan cheese. Cut in ½ cup butter till pieces are size of small peas. Sprinkle with water, stirring just till moistened. Form into a ball; press onto the bottom and 1½ inches up the sides of a 10-inch springform pan or a 10x2-inch round tart pan with a removable bottom. Bake in a 375° oven for 8 minutes. Remove from oven. ♦ Meanwhile, remove any skin and bones from salmon; flake into small pieces (you should have about *2 cups*). ♦ For filling, cook onion and garlic in 3 tablespoons butter till tender. In a bowl combine eggs, sour cream, and ¼ cup flour. Stir in salmon and onion mixture. Stir in *1 cup* of the Gruyère or Swiss cheese, dill, and ¼ teaspoon *salt*. ♦ Pour filling into the partially baked crust. Sprinkle with the remaining cheese. Bake in the 375° oven for 40 to 45 minutes or till a knife inserted near the center comes out clean, covering with foil the last 15 minutes. ♦ Cool pie in the pan for 15 minutes. Remove sides of pan. Makes 6 servings.

It's like stepping back into time—a wonderful, old, Southern mansion with a sweeping four-foot-wide staircase, polished pine floors covered with Persian rugs, elegant antiques from the Georgian and Regency periods, and European crystal chandeliers. **The Gastonian,** located in the romantic historic district of Savannah, Georgia, captures the luxurious and genteel charm of the 1800s. At the Gastonian, innkeepers Hugh and Roberta Lineberger believe that elegance and hospitality are closely tied. Among the many amenities Hugh and Roberta offer are wine, fresh fruit, and flowers upon arrival; afternoon tea in the elegant parlors; and a bountiful hot breakfast each morning.

SAUSAGE STRATA

1 pound bulk pork sausage
8 slices very thin white bread
1 tablespoon butter *or* margarine
1½ cups shredded sharp cheddar cheese (6 ounces)
3 beaten eggs
1¾ cups milk
¼ to ½ teaspoon bottled hot pepper sauce

In a large skillet cook sausage till no longer pink. Drain and discard juices. ♦ Trim crusts from bread. Discard crusts. Spread the butter or margarine on *one side* of *each* bread slice. ♦ To assemble, in an ungreased 8x8x2-inch baking dish place *four* of the bread slices, buttered sides up. Then sprinkle *half* of the sausage and *half* of the cheese on top of the bread. Repeat layering with remaining bread and sausage (set remaining cheese aside for later). ♦ In a medium mixing bowl combine eggs, milk, and hot pepper sauce. Pour egg mixture over layers in baking dish. Using a spatula, slightly press down on layers to moisten bread. Cover with plastic wrap and refrigerate for 2 to 24 hours. ♦ Remove plastic wrap from baking dish. Bake in a 325° oven for 35 to 40 minutes or till the center appears set and edges are lightly golden. *Immediately* sprinkle the remaining cheese on top. Let stand about 5 minutes or till cheese is melted. Makes 6 servings.

Nestled along the scenic St. Croix River Valley in Minnesota is a unique 1856 lumberman's mansion known as **The Asa Parker House.** Summer guests at this inn particularly enjoy canoeing on the sandbar-studded river. Innkeeper Marjorie Bush packs picnic breakfasts for canoeists who want to get an early start. Feasting on Bacon 'n' Wild Rice Egg Casseroles, juice, fruit, and freshly baked muffins in a quiet outdoor setting can be an unforgettable experience.

BACON 'N' WILD RICE EGG CASSEROLES

8 ounces sliced bacon
1 tablespoon butter *or* margarine
3 cups sliced fresh mushrooms (8 ounces)
1 small onion, chopped (⅓ cup)
¾ cup cooked wild rice
⅔ cup shredded Swiss cheese (about 3 ounces)
½ cup herb-seasoned stuffing mix
⅓ cup shredded Monterey Jack cheese (about 1½ ounces)
2 teaspoons snipped parsley
¼ teaspoon ground nutmeg
9 beaten eggs
1¼ cups whipping cream, light cream, *or* half-and-half

In a skillet cook bacon till crisp. Drain and reserve drippings. Crumble bacon; set aside. ◆ Use some of the drippings to lightly grease five 8- or 10-ounce casseroles or an 8x8x2-inch baking dish; set aside. ◆ Return *1 tablespoon* of the drippings to the skillet. Add butter to drippings in skillet. Add mushrooms and onion; cook till tender and most of the liquid is evaporated. ◆ In a bowl combine bacon, mushroom mixture, wild rice, Swiss cheese, stuffing mix, Monterey Jack cheese, parsley, nutmeg, ⅛ to ¼ teaspoon *salt,* and ⅛ teaspoon *pepper.* ◆ In another bowl combine eggs and cream. Pour egg mixture over rice mixture. Stir till combined. ◆ Transfer mixture to the prepared casseroles or baking dish. Bake, uncovered, in a 350° oven for 30 to 35 minutes for casseroles or 45 to 50 minutes for baking dish or till a knife inserted in centers comes out clean. Let stand 5 minutes before serving or prepare to tote as directed below. Serves 5 or 6.
◆ **To tote:** Prepare and bake mixture in casseroles. Wrap each casserole in *heavy* foil. Then wrap each in a *heavy* napkin, tying the napkin into a knot on top of the casserole. Pack in basket with juice, fruit, and muffins. Casseroles will stay warm about 40 minutes.

In the evening, the light will be on to welcome wedding couples at the **Park Row Bed & Breakfast.** Located 66 miles southwest of Minneapolis, Minnesota, the Victorian house provides a quiet escape.

Honeymoon couples stay in the German Room, which uses romantic pink as its theme color. The walls are covered with pink floral wallpaper and the bed is blanketed with a hand-embroidered pink bedspread. In the morning, innkeeper Ann L. Burckhardt honors the couple with a special breakfast, served in their room, featuring Honeymooners' Casseroles as the entrée.

HONEYMOONERS' CASSEROLES

1½ **cups refrigerated** *or* **frozen loose-pack hash brown potatoes**
½ **cup shredded Monterey Jack cheese with jalapeño peppers (2 ounces)**
½ **cup diced fully cooked ham**
½ **cup shredded Swiss cheese (2 ounces)**
2 **beaten eggs**
½ **cup light cream** *or* **half-and-half**

Thaw potatoes, if frozen. Then press the potatoes between paper towels to remove excess moisture. ♦ Grease two 8-ounce casseroles. Arrange potatoes evenly in the bottoms of the casseroles. Bake, uncovered, in a 400° oven for 20 minutes. Remove casseroles from oven and let stand about 10 minutes to cool slightly. Reduce oven temperature to 350°. ♦ On top of the potatoes in the casseroles, layer Montery Jack cheese, ham, and Swiss cheese. ♦ In a small mixing bowl combine the eggs and light cream or half-and-half. Pour egg mixture over potato-and-cheese mixture in casseroles. Bake, uncovered, in the 350° oven about 25 minutes or till centers appear set. Let stand about 5 minutes before serving. Makes 2 servings.

Named after a grand hotel in Dublin, Ireland, **The Shelburne Country Inn** in Seaview, Washington, has been a retreat for travelers since 1896. In 1977, innkeepers Laurie Anderson and David Campiche began a major refurnishing of the inn. One large project involved installing art nouveau windows, which had been salvaged from an old English church, in the restaurant's front dining room and pub. The light shimmering through these stained glass windows exemplifies the beauty of the past coming alive at the Shelburne.

BANANA PECAN PANCAKES

1 cup all-purpose flour
½ teaspoon baking soda
½ cup cornmeal
¼ cup oat bran
1 beaten egg
1½ cups buttermilk
1 ripe medium banana, mashed (⅓ cup)
2 tablespoons butter *or* margarine, melted
2 teaspoons honey
¼ cup chopped toasted pecans
1 recipe Cranberry-Orange Sauce *or* maple syrup

In a large bowl stir together flour, soda, and ¼ teaspoon *salt.* Stir in cornmeal and oat bran. ♦ In a bowl stir together egg, buttermilk, banana, butter, and honey. ♦ Add banana mixture to flour mixture. Stir just till moistened. Fold in pecans. ♦ Pour about ¼ *cup* batter for *each* pancake onto a hot, lightly greased griddle or heavy skillet. Spread each to about 4½ inches. Cook till golden brown, turning once. Serve with sauce or syrup. Makes 12 pancakes.

♦ **Cranberry-Orange Sauce:** In a saucepan stir together 1 cup *sugar* and ¾ cup *water.* Bring to boiling; add 3 cups *cranberries,* ¼ cup *dry white wine,* 1½ teaspoons finely shredded *orange peel,* 3 tablespoons *orange juice,* and 1 inch *stick cinnamon* or ¼ teaspoon *ground cinnamon.* Return to boiling; reduce heat. Simmer, uncovered, for 15 minutes. Remove from heat; remove and reserve cinnamon stick. Cool mixture slightly. Place mixture into a blender container or food processor bowl. Cover and blend or process about 30 seconds or till smooth. Return to saucepan and add reserved cinnamon stick. Simmer, uncovered, for 10 to 15 minutes or till slightly thickened. Serve warm. Makes about 2½ cups.

Called the castle by the townspeople of Bellevue, Iowa, the **Spring Side Inn** is perched on a high bluff overlooking the Mississippi River. The tall limestone structure with its Gothic Revival architecture resembles many of the castles and large homes in Europe. Guests at this inn certainly feel like kings and queens in any of the four large guest rooms. Each room has a panoramic view of the Mississippi, a queen-size bed, and a private bath. Innkeepers Mark and Nancy Jaspers further pamper their guests by placing fresh flowers, candies, and port wine in each of the rooms.

GINGERBREAD PANCAKES

1½ cups all-purpose flour
1 teaspoon baking powder
1 teaspoon ground cinnamon
½ teaspoon ground ginger
¼ teaspoon baking soda
¼ teaspoon salt
1 egg
1¼ cups milk
¼ cup molasses
3 tablespoons cooking oil
1 recipe Lemon Sauce

In a medium mixing bowl stir together the flour, baking powder, cinnamon, ginger, baking soda, and salt. ♦ In a large mixing bowl beat the egg and milk till combined. Then beat in molasses and cooking oil. ♦ Add the flour mixture to the milk mixture and stir just till blended but still slightly lumpy. ♦ Pour about *¼ cup* batter for *each* pancake onto a hot, lightly greased griddle or heavy skillet. Cook over medium heat till browned, turning to cook second sides when pancakes have bubbly surfaces and slightly dry edges. Serve with Lemon Sauce. Makes about 10 pancakes.

♦ **Lemon Sauce:** In a small saucepan stir together ½ cup *sugar*, 4 teaspoons *cornstarch*, and dash ground *nutmeg*. Stir in 1 cup *water*. Cook and stir till thickened and bubbly. Then cook and stir for 2 minutes more. Remove from heat. Add 2 tablespoons *butter* or *margarine*, ½ teaspoon finely shredded *lemon peel*, and 2 tablespoons *lemon juice*. Stir just till butter or margarine melts. Serve warm. Makes 1¼ cups.

Guests at **Lone Mountain Ranch** in Montana begin their active day with a gourmet breakfast served in the traditional western dining room in the lodge of this 23-guest-cabin ranch. Although the ranch provides recreational services such as horseback riding, fly fishing, and wilderness hikes in the summer, it is best known for its cross-country skiing in the winter. Forty-six miles of outstanding groomed ski trails, which wind through meadows, around ridges, and into mountain valleys, begin right outside the cabin doors. Or, for those who want to spend the day skiing into the wilderness of Yellowstone Park or Spanish Peaks, the Ranch provides guided tours.

HEAVENLY HOTS

½ **cup all-purpose flour**
4 **teaspoons sugar**
½ **teaspoon baking soda**
¼ **teaspoon salt**
2 **beaten eggs**
1 8-ounce **carton dairy sour cream**
Raspberry syrup *or* **raspberry sauce**

In a small mixing bowl stir together flour, sugar, baking soda, and salt. ♦ In a medium mixing bowl stir together beaten eggs and sour cream till combined. ♦ Add sour cream mixture to flour mixture. Use a wire whisk or rotary beater to beat just till blended but still slightly lumpy. If desired, cover and refrigerate batter overnight. ♦ Spoon a *generous 1 tablespoon* of batter for *each* silver-dollar-size pancake onto a hot, lightly greased griddle. Cook till golden brown, turning to cook second sides when the pancakes have bubbly surfaces and slightly dry edges. Serve with raspberry syrup or sauce. Makes 20 to 24 silver-dollar-size pancakes.

Imagine staying overnight in a museum-like home filled with original 18th-century furniture and accessories. It's possible at the **Villa de La Fontaine** in Charleston, South Carolina. The 1838 Greek Revival temple often is regarded as a museum by many guests.

Guest rooms are spacious and magnificent. Innkeeper William A. Fontaine has filled the rooms with museum-quality furnishings such as a Charleston rice bed with a beautiful canopy, a Philadelphia highboy from the 1770s, and a Chippendale secretary with seven secret

compartments. In the morning, guests enjoy breakfast in an elegant solarium that features a hand-painted mural and 12-foot arched Palladian windows. For the connoisseur of fine furnishings, an overnight stay at the Villa is a dream come true.

CORNMEAL WAFFLES

1 cup all-purpose flour
1 cup cornmeal
1 tablespoon baking powder
1 tablespoon sugar
½ teaspoon salt
2 cups milk
½ cup cooking oil
1 egg

In a large mixing bowl stir together flour, cornmeal, baking powder, sugar, and salt. ♦ In a medium mixing bowl beat milk, cooking oil, and egg till combined. Add milk mixture to flour mixture. Use a wire whisk or rotary beater to beat just till blended but still slightly lumpy. Let batter stand for 15 minutes. ♦ Pour ¾ *to 1 cup* batter onto the grids of a preheated, generously greased waffle baker. Close lid quickly; do not open during baking. Bake according to manufacturer's directions. When the waffle is done, use a fork to lift it off the grid. Repeat with remaining batter, stirring batter before pouring it onto the grids. Makes 16 (4-inch) waffles.

Innkeeper Anne Castle at **The Inn at Cedar Falls** in Ohio invites guests to pull up a kitchen stool and chat with her while she prepares her Fancy Stuffed French Toast for breakfast. Her informal hospitality makes new-comers soon feel at home in this completely restored 1840 log house. The inn provides guests with the simplicity of a rustic lodge yet has all of the modern niceties such as gourmet dining, private baths, thick towels, writing desks, and rocking chairs. Warm hospitality and a comfortable place to stay is what makes The Inn at Cedar Falls a home away from home.

FANCY STUFFED FRENCH TOAST

1 1-pound loaf unsliced French bread
1 8-ounce package cream cheese, softened
⅓ cup peach preserves
5 eggs
1¼ cups milk
½ teaspoon vanilla
¼ teaspoon ground cinnamon
Dash ground nutmeg
2 tablespoons butter *or* margarine
Maple syrup

Cut the French bread into *16 slices* (slices should be about 1 inch thick). Then cut a pocket in each slice, cutting from the top-crust side almost to the bottom-crust side. ◆ In a small mixing bowl stir together softened cream cheese and peach preserves. ◆ Spoon about *1 tablespoon* of the cheese mixture into *each* pocket. ◆ In a mixing bowl beat eggs, milk, vanilla, cinnamon, and nutmeg till combined. ◆ Dip stuffed bread slices into egg mixture. On a griddle or in a skillet heat butter or margarine. Add stuffed bread slices. Fry over medium heat till golden brown, turning once (allow about 1½ minutes for each side). Serve with maple syrup. Makes 16 slices.

Innkeeper Bill Oxford loves to tell the story about how his grandfather, Judge W. J. Oxford, Sr., was paid $3,000 in silver coins for winning a lawsuit. The judge toted these coins home in a box on the back of his buggy for the purpose of building **The Oxford House.** The desire to preserve the family history and restore the house led Bill and his wife Paula to innkeeping. Today, the four-guest-room house with its large porches and ginger-bread trim is the only house remaining in the Stephenville, Texas, area that features the Victorian grandeur of the 1890s. By furnishing their inn with family memorabilia such as photographs, charcoal portraits, hats, gloves, antique dolls, and early-1900s letters, the Oxfords help guests experience the love and history that make this house so special.

BAKED VICTORIAN FRENCH TOAST

1 cup packed brown sugar
⅓ cup butter *or* margarine
2 tablespoons light corn syrup
4 slices Texas toast *or* 6 ¾-inch-thick slices of French bread (5 to 6 ounces total)
5 eggs
1½ cups milk
1 teaspoon ground cinnamon
Strawberries, peaches, *or* pears, sliced, *or* blueberries *or* raspberries (optional)
Powdered sugar (optional)

In a small saucepan cook and stir brown sugar, butter or margarine, and light corn syrup just till butter or margarine is melted. Pour brown sugar mixture into an ungreased 12x7½x2-inch baking dish. Arrange bread slices in a single layer on top of the brown sugar mixture. If necessary, cut bread to fit into dish. Set baking dish aside. ♦ In a medium mixing bowl beat eggs, milk, and cinnamon till combined. Pour egg mixture over bread in baking dish. Cover and refrigerate for 2 to 24 hours. ♦ Remove the cover from the baking dish. Bake in a 350° oven for 30 to 35 minutes or till the center appears set and the top is lightly browned. Let the French toast stand about 10 minutes before serving. If desired, top with fruit and/or sift powdered sugar over top. Makes 4 or 6 slices.

As travelers stroll through the historic Oakwood District of Raleigh, North Carolina, they'll come upon **The Oakwood Inn** tucked in a beautiful 20-block area of restored Victorian homes. Built in 1871 by Kenneth C. Raynon, a North Carolina delegate to the Constitutional Convention, the home is listed in the National Register of Historic Places. Restored with historical detail and graced with vintage Victorian antiques, The Oakwood Inn is true to its period in both ambience and service. Upon arrival, guests are greeted with homemade refreshments. For special romantic occasions, champagne, roses, and chocolates are placed in the guests' room. Each morning, guests are treated to an elaborate breakfast buffet served on an Eastlake Gothic sideboard in the formal dining room. Lace curtains and beautiful china and silver help complete the Victorian scene.

BAKED PECAN FRENCH TOAST

4 eggs
⅔ cup orange juice
⅓ cup milk
¼ cup sugar
½ teaspoon vanilla
¼ teaspoon ground nutmeg
8 ½-inch-thick slices Italian *or* French bread
¼ cup butter *or* margarine
½ cup chopped pecans
1 recipe Orange Syrup

Beat eggs, juice, milk, sugar, vanilla, and nutmeg till combined. ♦ In a 13x9x2-inch baking dish arrange bread slices in a single layer. Pour egg mixture over bread. Cover; refrigerate 2 to 24 hours. ♦ Place butter in a 15x10x1-inch baking pan. Place in a preheating 350° oven just till butter is melted. Remove from oven; tilt pan to spread butter over bottom. ♦ Place bread slices in a single layer on top of melted butter. ♦ Bake in a 350° oven 20 minutes. Sprinkle with pecans. Bake 10 minutes more or till nuts are lightly toasted and toast is golden. Serve with Orange Syrup. Makes 8 slices.
♦ **Orange Syrup:** In a small saucepan combine ½ cup *butter* or *margarine*, ½ cup *sugar*, and ½ of a 6-ounce can (⅓ cup) frozen *orange juice concentrate*. Cook and stir over low heat till butter or margarine is melted. *Do not boil*. Remove from heat and cool for 10 minutes. Using a rotary beater, beat till slightly thickened. Serve warm. Makes ¾ cup.

As the brochure for **The Inn at Union Pier** reads, this inn is the place to "discover the meaning of relaxation." Located in Michigan just 1½ hours from Chicago, The Inn at Union Pier is a popular beachside retreat for Chicagoans trying to escape the hectic city life. With Lake Michigan only 200 steps from the door, guests are able to enjoy a walk on the beach with the inn's dog, Sandy. Boating, fishing, swimming, windsurfing, and sunbathing also are popular pastimes. Winter fun includes cross-county skiing and tobogganing. If guests prefer a more quiet day, they can choose to play a game of croquet or boccie ball, visit antique shops and galleries, or just put up their feet and relax on the comfortable chaise longues.

POPOVERS ROMANOFF

Nonstick spray coating *or* 1 tablespoon shortening
1 cup milk
2 eggs
1 tablespoon butter *or* margarine, melted
1 cup all-purpose flour
¼ teaspoon salt
3 cups strawberries, halved
1 recipe Romanoff Sauce

Prepare Romanoff Sauce. ◆ Spray six 6-ounce custard cups with nonstick coating or grease the bottom and sides of *each* cup with *½ teaspoon* of shortening. Place cups on a 15x10x1-inch baking pan. Set pan aside. ◆ In a medium mixing bowl beat milk, eggs, and melted butter or margarine till combined. Add flour and salt. Beat till smooth. ◆ Fill the prepared cups *half* full with batter. ◆ Bake in a 400° oven about 40 minutes or till very firm and crusts are glossy and golden brown. ◆ *Immediately* after removing popovers from the oven, use the tines of a fork to prick each popover to let the steam escape. Turn oven off. For crisper popovers, return popovers to oven for 5 to 10 minutes. ◆ Remove popovers from cups. To serve, place popovers on small plates. Top with strawberries and sauce. Serves 6.
◆ **Romanoff Sauce:** In a small bowl stir together 1½ cups dairy *sour cream*, 2 tablespoons *powdered sugar*, 2 tablespoons *brown sugar*, 1 tablespoon *rum*, 1 teaspoon finely shredded *orange peel*, ½ teaspoon ground *cinnamon*, and ¼ teaspoon ground *nutmeg* till combined. Cover and refrigerate for up to 24 hours to let flavors blend. Makes about 1½ cups.

The **Colonel Ludlow Inn,** in the historic West End of Winston-Salem, North Carolina, blends yesteryear's charm with today's modern conveniences. Guests often are surprised to find luxuries such as two-person whirlpool baths, stereo systems with an assortment of tapes, coffee makers, small refrigerators, and 33-channel televisions hidden in a Victorian decor of alcoves, high ceilings, stained-glass windows, and period furnishings. This posh bed-and-breakfast is a haven for weary business travelers during the week and a romantic getaway for couples on weekends.

BACON-CHEDDAR MUFFINS

1¾ cups all-purpose flour
½ cup shredded sharp cheddar cheese (2 ounces)
¼ cup sugar
2 teaspoons baking powder
¼ teaspoon ground red pepper
1 beaten egg
¾ cup milk
⅓ cup cooking oil
6 slices bacon, crisp-cooked, drained,
and crumbled (⅓ cup)

Grease eight 2½-inch muffin cups *and* the top surface of the pan. Set muffin pan aside. ♦ In a medium bowl stir together the flour, cheddar cheese, sugar, baking powder, and ground red pepper. Make a well in the center of the flour mixture. ♦ In a small mixing bowl stir together the egg, milk, and cooking oil. Add egg mixture all at once to flour mixture. Stir just till moistened (batter should be lumpy). Fold in crumbled bacon. ♦ Spoon batter into the prepared muffin cups so batter is *even with the top* of the pan. ♦ Bake in a 400° oven for 20 to 25 minutes or till muffins are golden. Let stand for 3 to 5 minutes in the muffin cups. Then remove muffins from muffin cups. Serve warm. Makes 8 muffins.

It started as a dream for Frank and Judi Daley. After traveling and staying in bed-and-breakfasts, they became enamored with the idea of operating their own inn. That dream became a reality in 1986 when they purchased and restored a graceful Queen Anne-style home in Winter Park, Florida. **The Fortnightly Inn** is furnished with antiques from the Empire period and with Daley family heirlooms. At The Fortnightly Inn, guests are pampered with gourmet breakfasts in the elegant dining room, complimentary cream sherry in each of the five guest rooms and suites, home-baked cookies and tea or lemonade upon arrival, and luxurious bath amenities.

PEACH DELIGHT BRAN MUFFINS

Nonstick spray coating (optional)
1½ cups whole bran cereal buds
1 cup whole bran cereal shreds
½ cup light *or* dark raisins
¾ cup sugar
¾ cup buttermilk
¼ cup cooking oil
1 egg
1¼ cups all-purpose flour
1 teaspoon baking soda
½ teaspoon salt
½ cup chopped, peeled fresh peaches
or* chopped canned peaches, drained

Spray eighteen 2½-inch muffin cups with nonstick coating or line muffin cups with paper bake cups; set aside. ♦ In a small bowl combine bran buds, bran shreds, and raisins. Pour ½ cup *boiling water* over mixture; let stand for 5 to 10 minutes. ♦ Meanwhile, in a large bowl beat together sugar, buttermilk, cooking oil, and egg till combined. ♦ In a small bowl stir together flour, baking soda, and salt. Add flour mixture to egg mixture. Stir just till moistened. Stir in bran mixture. Fold in peaches. ♦ Spoon batter into the prepared muffin cups, filling each ¾ full. Bake in a 350° oven about 20 minutes or till tops spring back when lightly touched. ♦ Makes 18 muffins.
♦ *Teri Beasley, manager and gourmet cook at The Fortnightly Inn, suggests substituting fresh *blueberries* or *raspberries,* or chopped, peeled *pineapple, apples,* or *apricots* for the peaches.

In keeping with the European tradition of a bed-and-breakfast, only one meal, breakfast or brunch, is served at the **Grant Corner Inn** in downtown Santa Fe, New Mexico. This applause-worthy morning meal, served in the inn's cozy dining room, or on the front veranda in summer months, always starts with fresh fruit juice, a fruit frappé, or an in-season fresh fruit. There is usually a choice of two special entrées, such as cheese-chorizo strata or Belgian waffles with crème fraîche. A basket filled with a variety of breads comes with every entrée. These Chocolate-Orange Muffins and French Apple-Butter Muffins are just two of the many muffins, coffee cakes, breads, and pastries innkeepers Louise S. Stewart and Martin (Pat) S. Walter of the Grant Corner Inn serve to their guests.

CHOCOLATE-ORANGE MUFFINS

1 cup sugar
½ cup unsalted butter, softened
2 eggs
2 tablespoons finely shredded orange peel
½ cup dairy sour cream
½ cup orange juice
2 cups all-purpose flour
¾ teaspoon baking powder
½ teaspoon salt
½ teaspoon baking soda
3 squares (3 ounces) semisweet chocolate, chopped

Line eighteen 2½-inch muffin cups with paper bake cups. Set muffin cups aside. ♦ In a large mixing bowl beat sugar and butter with an electric mixer on medium to high speed till well creamed. Beat in eggs and orange peel till combined. Then beat in sour cream and orange juice just till combined. ♦ In a small mixing bowl stir together flour, baking powder, salt, and soda. Gently stir flour mixture into butter mixture just till combined. Fold in chocolate. ♦ Spoon batter into the prepared muffin cups, filling each ¾ full. Bake in a 375° oven about 20 minutes or till a wooden toothpick inserted near each center comes out clean. Makes 18 muffins.

(Grant Corner Inn, continued)

FRENCH APPLE-BUTTER MUFFINS

½ cup sugar
6 tablespoons unsalted butter, softened
½ cup milk
1 egg
1½ cups all-purpose flour
2 teaspoons baking powder
½ teaspoon ground nutmeg
¼ teaspoon salt
¼ cup apple butter
¼ cup sugar
½ teaspoon ground cinnamon
¼ cup unsalted butter, melted

Line twelve 2½-inch muffin cups with paper bake cups. Set muffin cups aside. ◆ In a medium mixing bowl beat the ½ cup sugar and the 6 tablespoons butter with an electric mixer on medium to high speed till well creamed. Beat in milk and egg. ◆ In a small mixing bowl stir together the flour, baking powder, nutmeg, and salt. Gently stir the flour mixture into the butter mixture just till combined. ◆ Divide batter in half. Using 1 portion of the batter, spoon batter evenly into the prepared muffin cups. ◆ Make a depression in batter in each cup. Then spoon *1 teaspoon* of apple butter into *each* depression. Using the remaining portion of batter, spoon batter evenly on top of the apple butter in the muffin cups. ◆ Bake in a 350° oven for 20 to 25 minutes or till muffin tops are golden brown. Remove muffins from muffin cups and let stand for 5 minutes to cool slightly. Combine ¼ cup sugar and cinnamon. Dip the tops of muffins in ¼ cup melted butter; roll in sugar-cinnamon mixture. Serve warm. Makes 12 muffins.

When innkeeper Marjorie Martin of the **Peppertrees Bed & Breakfast Inn** first arrived in America from England, she was confused by coffee cake because it did not have a coffee flavor. So Marjorie, who loves coffee but not chocolate, developed her own recipe. By adding finely ground coffee to a chocolate chip coffee cake and by substituting vanilla-flavored pieces for chocolate pieces, Marjorie created the Peppertrees' Coffee Coffee Cake.

This coffee-flavored coffee cake is just one of the many delicious breads that can be enjoyed at the Peppertrees Bed & Breakfast Inn. In fact, each morning at this turn-of-the-century southwestern home in Tucson, Arizona, Marjorie greets her guests with a big pot of tea or coffee and freshly baked bread.

PEPPERTREES' COFFEE COFFEE CAKE

2½ teaspoons instant coffee crystals
1 cup buttermilk
2½ cups all-purpose flour
½ cup packed brown sugar
¼ cup butter *or* margarine
1 cup vanilla-flavored pieces
½ cup chopped nuts
1 cup sugar
½ cup butter *or* margarine, softened
2 eggs
1 teaspoon vanilla
1 teaspoon baking powder
½ teaspoon baking soda

Grease a 13x9x2-inch baking pan; set aside. Stir *1½ teaspoons* of the coffee crystals into the buttermilk; set aside. ♦ For topping, in a small mixing bowl stir together *½ cup* of the flour, the brown sugar, and the remaining 1 teaspoon coffee crystals. Cut in the ¼ cup butter or margarine till the mixture resembles coarse crumbs. Then stir in *½ cup* of the vanilla-flavored pieces and the chopped nuts. Set topping aside. ♦ For batter, in a large mixing bowl beat sugar and the ½ cup butter or margarine with an electric mixer on medium to high speed till well creamed. Add the eggs, one at a time, beating till well combined. Then beat in vanilla. ♦ In another small mixing bowl stir together the remaining 2 cups flour, baking powder, and baking soda. Alternately beat flour mixture and buttermilk mixture into the sugar-batter mixture. Stir in the remaining ½ cup vanilla-flavored pieces. ♦ Evenly spread batter into the prepared baking pan, smoothing top. Sprinkle topping over batter. Bake in a 350° oven about 35 minutes or till a wooden toothpick inserted near the center comes out clean. Let stand about 10 minutes to cool slightly before serving. Makes 16 servings.

♦ **Peppertrees' Chocolate Coffee Cake:** Prepare the Peppertrees' Coffee Coffee Cake as directed above, *except* omit the instant coffee crystals from the buttermilk and the topping. Stir 2 teaspoons unsweetened *cocoa powder* into the topping. ♦ Use 1 cup *semisweet chocolate pieces* instead of the 1 cup vanilla-flavored pieces in the topping and batter.

The personal charm and beautiful character of **The Norris House Inn** in the historic district of Leesburg, Virginia, makes it a perfect place for celebrating special occasions such as small wedding receptions and family reunions. At this 1806 Federal-style house, breakfast is served by candlelight in the inn's handsome dining room. Walton's Mountain Coffee Cake, named after former innkeeper Laura Walton, has become a favorite among guests. For a buffet breakfast, the cake is usually inverted onto a silver tray, and placed on a beautiful mahogany sideboard.

WALTON'S MOUNTAIN COFFEE CAKE

½ **cup pecan halves**
2 15-ounce packages frozen white dinner-roll dough
(18 to 24 dough balls total)
1 4-serving-size package *instant* **butterscotch pudding mix**
1 cup packed brown sugar
½ **cup butter** *or* **margarine**
⅛ **teaspoon ground cinnamon**

Generously grease a 10-inch fluted tube pan. Sprinkle pecans in the bottom of the pan. Arrange the *frozen* dough balls on top of the pecans. Sprinkle pudding mix over dough balls. ◆ In a small saucepan cook and stir brown sugar, butter or margarine, and cinnamon till butter is melted. Pour butter mixture over pudding mix and dough balls in the tube pan. Cover and refrigerator for 12 to 24 hours. ◆ Uncover and bake in a 350° oven about 30 minutes or till top is golden brown. *Immediately* invert coffee cake onto a serving tray or plate. Let stand about 15 minutes to cool slightly before serving. Makes 12 servings.

In the mountains of North Carolina, guests of the **Mast Farm Inn** experience the down-home hospitality common in the past. The 19th-century farmstead includes a big farmhouse and numerous out-buildings (springhouse, woodshed, icehouse, large barn, blacksmith's shop, woodworking shop, and gazebo). Innkeepers Sibyl and Francis Pressly created the back-in-time feeling by furnishing the restored 1885 home with turn-of-the-century antiques and by serving meals that are feasts. In the mornings, guests are treated to hearty breakfasts of fresh fruits; homemade breads and jams; and pancakes, breakfast casseroles, or the inn's favorite—stuffed French toast. In the evenings, Sibyl and Francis serve family-style portions of country foods along with in-season salad greens and vegetables from their garden. Generous portions of home-cooked food, a warm atmosphere, and simple furnishings indeed make guests feel as though they've walked into a quieter, gentler time.

APRICOT-CHEESE COFFEE CAKE

3 cups packaged biscuit mix
2 tablespoons brown sugar
½ cup milk
¼ cup margarine *or* butter, melted
1 cup ricotta cheese
1 3-ounce package cream cheese, softened
2 eggs
⅓ cup sugar
1 teaspoon vanilla
½ to 1 cup apricot preserves *or* seedless red raspberry jam

In a medium mixing bowl stir together biscuit mix and brown sugar. Make a well in the center of the dry mixture. Add milk and melted margarine or butter. Stir just till moistened. ♦ Turn dough out onto a lightly floured surface. Quickly knead dough by gently folding and pressing dough for 15 strokes. ♦ Press dough onto the bottom and 1 inch up the sides of an ungreased 9x9x2-inch baking pan. If desired, cover and chill overnight. ♦ For filling, in a medium mixing bowl beat ricotta cheese and cream cheese with an electric mixer till combined. Add eggs, sugar, and vanilla. Beat till smooth. ♦ Pour filling onto the unbaked biscuit crust. Bake in a 350° oven about 35 minutes or till center appears set and edges of crust are golden. ♦ Stir preserves or jam, then spread on top of coffee cake. Let stand about 20 minutes to cool slightly before serving. Serves 9.

Situated on top of a hill overlooking the wine-growing region of Sonoma County in California is a three-story mansion called **Madrona Manor.** At the Madrona Manor, guests are treated to the elegance and fine dining of country inns found in Europe. A simple European-style breakfast buffet of fresh orange juice, seasonal fruit, assorted cheeses and cold meats, eggs, cold cereals, toast, and freshly brewed coffee is served in the Victorian, parlorlike dining room. Near the end of breakfast, guests are offered Churros, Madrona Manor's signature breakfast pastry. These fried, eclairlike pastries are served with homemade kiwi, raspberry, and orange preserves.

CHURROS

⅓ **cup butter *or* margarine**
1 cup all-purpose flour
1 tablespoon sugar
⅛ **teaspoon salt**
4 eggs
¼ **teaspoon vanilla**
Cooking oil *or* shortening for deep-fat frying
Powdered sugar ♦ Assorted preserves

In a medium saucepan combine 1 cup *water* and butter. Bring to boiling, stirring till butter or margarine melts. Then add flour, sugar, and salt all at once, stirring vigorously with a wooden spoon. Cook and stir till mixture forms a ball that doesn't separate. Remove from the heat and cool for 10 minutes. ♦ Add eggs, one at a time, to the butter mixture, beating with the wooden spoon after each addition about 1 minute or till smooth. Stir in vanilla. ♦ In a heavy saucepan or deep-fat fryer heat 2 inches of oil or melted shortening to 375°. Spoon dough into a decorating bag fitted with a large star tip (¾-inch opening). Holding the bag about 3 inches over hot fat, carefully pipe 2-inch strips of dough, a few at a time, into the hot fat. (To easily make even-size pieces, cut the dough with kitchen scissors after piping a 2-inch strip.) ♦ Fry for 1 to 2 minutes or till puffy and golden. Use a slotted spoon to remove pastries from hot fat. Drain on paper towels. Sift powdered sugar over pastries. Serve warm. (To eat, break open and fill the middle with preserves.) Makes about 40.

Guests feel right at home at the **Swedish Country Inn** with its lace curtains, Swedish pine furnishings, and cupboards and window trim painted with delicate flowers in Dalacarlian style (a Swedish folk-art technique). The inn is located in Lindsborg, a small central-Kansas community that calls itself "Little Sweden" and still retains many of its Swedish traditions. At the Swedish Country Inn, guests enjoy a full Scandinavian buffet breakfast, which includes Swedish delicacies such as Kringler (a frosted pastry), pickled herring, hardtack, hard-cooked eggs, cold cuts, and cheeses.

KRINGLER

1 cup *cold* butter *or* margarine
2 cups all-purpose flour
1 to 2 tablespoons *cold* water
3 eggs
½ teaspoon almond extract
1 cup sifted powdered sugar
1 tablespoon butter *or* margarine, melted
Few drops almond extract
Light cream, half-and-half, *or* milk

In a bowl cut *½ cup* of the butter into *1 cup* of the flour till pieces are the size of small peas. ♦ Sprinkle with *1 teaspoon* of the water, then gently toss with a fork. Push moistened dough to side of bowl. Add additional water, 1 teaspoon at a time, till all is moistened. Form dough into a ball. Divide ball in half. ♦ On an ungreased baking sheet pat or roll *each* portion of dough into a 12x4-inch strip; set aside. ♦ For top layer, in a medium saucepan combine 1 cup *water* and the remaining butter. Bring to boiling, stirring till butter melts. Add the remaining flour all at once, stirring vigorously. Cool for 10 minutes. Add eggs, one at a time, beating with a wooden spoon after each addition. Stir in the ½ teaspoon almond extract. ♦ Spread top layer mixture evenly over each pastry strip. Bake in a 375° oven about 40 minutes or till puffy and golden. ♦ Remove from baking sheet and cool on wire racks. Stir together the powdered sugar, 1 tablespoon butter or margarine, a few drops of almond extract, and enough light cream to make a frosting of drizzling consistency. Drizzle over pastries. To serve, cut pastries diagonally into 1-inch slices. Makes 16 servings.
♦ **Note:** To store, place *unfrosted* pastries in a covered airtight container in the freezer. To serve, thaw and frost as directed above.

After a long day at work, business travelers especially will appreciate the first-class accommodations and personal service offered at the **Millsaps Buie House**. This 1888 stately mansion in Jackson, Mississippi, has 11 guest rooms comfortably furnished with a mixture of antiques and period-piece reproductions. Each room features a telephone with computer dataport, cable television, and a private bath. Other amenities include an on-site fax machine and daily newspapers. As an additional convenience, the staff of three innkeepers cheerfully provides services such as taking telephone messages and sending personal laundry out for cleaning.

PECAN HORNS

1 cup *cold* butter, cut up
1 8-ounce package cream cheese, cut up
2 cups all-purpose flour
⅔ cup sugar
1 tablespoon ground cinnamon
¼ cup butter, melted
1¼ cups finely chopped pecans
¾ cup chopped raisins
1 recipe Powdered Sugar Glaze

In a mixing bowl cut the 1 cup butter and cream cheese into flour till pieces are the size of coarse crumbs. Divide and press mixture into 3 balls. ♦ In a small bowl stir together sugar and cinnamon; set aside. ♦ On a lightly floured surface, slightly flatten 1 dough ball. Then roll dough into a 13-inch circle. Brush with some of the ¼ cup melted butter. Sprinkle with *one-third* of *each* of the sugar-cinnamon mixture, pecans, and raisins. Cut circle into 12 wedges. Roll up wedges, starting at the wide ends and rolling toward points. Place pastries, point sides down, on ungreased baking sheets. Repeat with remaining dough, melted butter, sugar-cinnamon mixture, pecans, and raisins. ♦ Bake in a 350° oven for 18 to 20 minutes or till bottoms are golden. Remove from baking sheets and cool on wire racks. Drizzle glaze over tops. Makes 36.
♦ **Powdered Sugar Glaze:** In a small bowl stir together 1 cup sifted *powdered sugar*, ½ teaspoon *vanilla*, and 1 to 2 tablespoons *milk* to make a glaze of drizzling consistency. Makes ⅓ cup.
♦ **Note:** To make ahead, prepare and shape as directed above, but *do not bake*. Place Pecan Horns in a single layer on a baking sheet. Freeze, then remove from baking sheet and place in a freezer bag. Close bag, label, and freeze. To serve, place *frozen* Pecan Horns on baking sheets and bake as directed above. Drizzle glaze over tops.

The Newcastle Inn in Newcastle, Maine

New England Summer Breakfast

New England hospitality is at its best at the cozy Newcastle Inn. Located in Newcastle, Maine, the inn pampers its guests with gourmet American food, attractive surroundings, and a taste of the genteel life-style.

Freshly Squeezed Orange Juice

Blueberry Lemon Bread (page 45)

Strawberries with Crème

  Fraîche (page 46)

Ricotta Cheese Pies (page 47)

Sautéed Ham

Coffee

The Newcastle Inn charms its guests with outstanding hospitality, a beautiful setting, and creative cuisine.

When innkeepers Chris and Ted Sprague bought the 15-room inn in 1987, they set out to provide the standard of hospitality they demanded as inn goers. In fact, they didn't buy the inn until after they'd visited nearly 100 inns, attended seminars and read about innkeeping, and worked with a consultant.

They began their pursuit of quality and excellence by capitalizing on Chris' love of cooking and decorating and Ted's building and gardening skills.

Ted whipped the building and grounds of the 150-year-old Federal-style colonial inn into shape, and Chris breathed new life into the inn's decor.

The kitchen and the inn's cuisine especially have benefited from Chris' talent for balancing cooking trends with familiar tastes, a skill she developed while working in her family's gourmet food store as a youngster. As Ted says, "She takes the regular, and does unusual things with it."

The cuisine at The Newcastle Inn is definitely American, with a strong emphasis on fresh, high-quality ingredients. Maine products, like the state's famous blueberries or seafood, are favorite ingredients.

To assure their emphasis on freshness and quality is maintained, Chris and Ted contract with local farmers who custom-grow vegetables and fruits for the inn. A local fish market provides the seafood.

Whether guests sample a sumptuous breakfast or dinner at The Newcastle Inn, they leave with a delightful taste of New England-style hospitality.

"She takes the regular, and does unusual things with it." The cuisine is definitely American, with a strong emphasis on fresh, high-quality ingredients.

A four-course breakfast at The Newcastle Inn, which sometimes is served on the

screened porch, begins with juice followed by a bread, fruit, and entrée.

BLUEBERRY LEMON BREAD
(Pictured on pages 42–43)

¾ **cup sugar**
6 tablespoons butter *or* **margarine, softened**
2 eggs
4 teaspoons finely shredded lemon peel (set aside)
1 teaspoon lemon juice
2 cups all-purpose flour
1 tablespoon baking powder
¼ **teaspoon salt**
¾ **cup milk**
1 cup fresh *or* **frozen small blueberries***

Grease and flour two 7½x3½x2-inch loaf pans. Set loaf pans aside. ♦ In a large mixing bowl beat sugar and butter or margarine with an electric mixer on medium to high speed till well combined. Beat in eggs and lemon juice. ♦ In a small bowl stir together flour, baking powder, and salt. ♦ Alternately add flour mixture and milk to butter mixture, beating just till combined after each addition. Fold in blueberries and lemon peel. ♦ Spread batter evenly in the prepared loaf pans. Bake in a 350° oven for 40 to 45 minutes or till a wooden toothpick inserted near each center comes out clean. Cool bread in pans for 10 minutes. Then remove bread from the pans and cool on a wire rack. Makes 2 loaves.
♦ *Chris uses Maine blueberries in this bread. These blueberries often are smaller than the blueberries found in the supermarket. Because large berries will sink to the bottom of the bread, try to select the smallest berries possible.

Chris' background in gourmet foods is reflected in her cooking.

STRAWBERRIES WITH CRÈME FRAÎCHE

(Pictured on pages 42–43)

½ cup whipping cream
½ cup dairy sour cream
4 cups fresh strawberries, halved
¼ cup packed brown sugar

For the crème fraîche, in a small mixing bowl stir together the whipping cream and sour cream. Cover with plastic wrap and let stand at room temperature for 5 to 12 hours or till mixture thickens. When thickened, refrigerate for 24 hours. ♦ To serve, place strawberries in individual bowls. Top with crème fraîche, then sprinkle with brown sugar. Makes 6 to 8 servings.

Editor's Tip: Open your door and welcome your guests as an innkeeper would. Innkeepers have a reputation for turning even a short visit into a fond memory. Here are some ideas I've gathered on how you, too, can make your guests' stay special. ♦ Hang a few colorful balloons with ribbon on your mailbox in celebration of their arrival. ♦ In the winter, simmer potpourri on the stove or light a fire in the fireplace to give your home a warm feel. ♦ Place freshly cut flowers in a country pitcher on the bedside table. ♦ Fill an antique porcelain cup or small bowl with gold-foil-wrapped chocolates and place it on the dresser. ♦ Bid your guests a hearty good-bye with a small basket or decorative bag filled with nuts, dried fruits, cheeses, crackers, and beverages. You might want to add a small travel game if there are children.

RICOTTA CHEESE PIES
(Pictured on pages 42–43)

1 8-ounce package cream cheese, softened
3 egg yolks
1 15-ounce carton ricotta cheese (about 2 cups)
⅓ cup sugar
1 tablespoon vanilla
1 tablespoon Grand Marnier (optional)
1½ teaspoons finely shredded orange peel
12 18x12-inch sheets frozen phyllo dough, thawed
¾ cup unsalted butter, melted
Powdered sugar

For filling, in a medium mixing bowl beat cream cheese with an electric mixer till fluffy. Add egg yolks and beat till combined. Then add ricotta cheese, sugar, vanilla, and, if desired, Grand Marnier. Beat till thoroughly combined, scraping the sides of the bowl occasionally. Fold in orange peel. ♦ To assemble pies, unfold phyllo dough. Place 1 sheet of the phyllo dough on a waxed-paper-lined cutting board. (Cover the remaining phyllo dough with a damp towel to prevent it from drying out, then set it aside.) Fold the sheet of phyllo dough crosswise in half. Generously brush with some of the melted butter. Place *¼ cup* of the filling in a 3-inch-long strip about 2 inches from a long edge of the folded phyllo sheet. Fold the edge over the filling, then fold in sides. Continue folding to form a packet about 4 inches long and 2 inches wide. Repeat with remaining phyllo, some of the melted butter, and cheese mixture. ♦ Place the pies, seam sides down, in an ungreased 15x10x1-inch baking pan. Brush tops with remaining melted butter. Bake in a 375° oven about 15 minutes or till golden. Sift powdered sugar over the tops of the pies. Serve warm. Makes 12 servings.
♦ **Note:** To make ahead, prepare and assemble as directed above, but *do not bake.* Place pies in a single layer in a covered airtight container. Refrigerate for up to 24 hours or freeze for up to 3 months. To serve, place pies on an ungreased 15x10x1-inch baking pan. Bake in a 375° oven till golden, allowing about 15 minutes for refrigerated pies or 20 to 25 minutes for frozen pies. Serve as above.

*Washington School Inn
in Park City, Utah*

Skiers' Breakfast Buffet

Thanks to the dream of Frank O'Bryan, a California investor, and a Utah developer, a century-old former school building has found new life as an inn. Washington School, one of Park City's historical treasures, nearly disappeared due to neglect. But now, lovingly restored as an inn, the Washington School Inn welcomes dozens of visitors each week. With well-appointed guest rooms and a hearty breakfast buffet, the inn makes guests feel right at home. Located just 35 miles from Salt Lake City, the Washington School Inn sits in the heart of one of Utah's major ski areas and often serves as home base for winter vacationers. During the summer, golf, tennis, horseback riding, and fishing are available to the inn's guests.

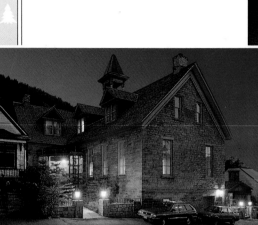

All the homey dishes are made from scratch. "It's a real typical American breakfast—very hearty."

Washington School Inn's Park City location makes it a favorite overnight stop for skiers flocking to Utah's mountain peaks and vacationers heading to nearby national parks. Guests love the inn's hearty breakfasts as well as the charming hospitality of manager Nancy Beaufait and innkeepers Delphine Covington, Karen Guthrie, and Cathy Elliott.

Originally a three-room schoolhouse, Washington School was built in 1889. More classrooms were added in 1903 and 1906. During the school's lifetime, it has survived 30 years of neglect and other hardships— everything from a major fire in 1898 to threatened demolition during Park City's modern building boom. The school was saved from an uncertain future when it opened in 1985 as an inn, following two years of restoration and renovation.

Now listed on the Utah State Register and National Register of Historic Places, the handsome limestone building has a sophisticated elegance. Its 15 guest rooms, each named after one of the school's former teachers, are decorated with antiques and country-style fabrics.

After a peaceful night's rest, guests can indulge in the inn's breakfast buffet. The breakfast menu changes daily so even on an extended stay, guests can sample something new every morning.

All the homey dishes on the special breakfast buffet are traditional favorites and are made from scratch in the inn's own kitchen. "It's a real typical American breakfast—very hearty," says Nancy.

After breakfast, if guests aren't in the mood for skiing or one of the other recreational options, they can relax in the hot tub, catch up on their reading in the library, play a board game, watch television, or stop by the kitchen for some freshly baked cookies. All in all, visitors can find lots of diversions at this Park City haven.

Apples and brown sugar add a pleasant sweetness to the pork sausage.

SKIERS' SAUSAGE
(Pictured on pages 48–49)

**1 pound fresh pork sausage links
6 medium cooking apples, cored and
each cut into 8 wedges (2 pounds total)
3 tablespoons brown sugar
1 tablespoon lemon juice
¼ teaspoon salt
⅛ teaspoon pepper**

In a large 12-inch skillet cook sausage over medium heat about 10 minutes or till no longer pink. Drain and discard juices. Cut sausage links crosswise in half. ♦ Return sausage links to the skillet. Add apple wedges. Then sprinkle with brown sugar, lemon juice, salt, and pepper. ♦ Cover and cook over medium-low heat for 10 to 15 minutes or till apples are just tender, gently stirring once or twice. Makes 6 servings.

***E**ditor's Tip: The buffet, an easy serving method for large groups, is often used at inns. Guests help themselves to food at the buffet table before seating themselves at smaller tables. If you want to serve buffet-style but your dining space is limited, arrange card tables in another room in the house. ♦ To arrange a buffet table for the Skiers' Breakfast Buffet, first set out plates, the French Toast Strata, and the Apple Cider Syrup. Then follow with the Skiers' Sausage, muffins, mixed fruit with yogurt, assorted cereals, and cereal bowls. Place beverages on a separate table or serve them from a tray after the guests are seated.*

The Stuffed French Toast Strata is definitely one of the guests' favorites, according

to Nancy. She says they're always requesting a copy of this recipe.

STUFFED FRENCH TOAST STRATA
(Pictured on pages 48–49)

1 1-pound loaf unsliced French bread
1 8-ounce package cream cheese, cubed
8 eggs
2½ cups milk, light cream, *or* half-and-half
6 tablespoons butter *or* margarine, melted
¼ cup maple syrup
1 recipe Apple Cider Syrup (see opposite page)

Cut French bread loaf into cubes. (You should have about *12 cups* bread cubes.) Grease a 13x9x2-inch baking dish. ♦ To assemble, in the prepared baking dish place *half* of the bread cubes. Top with the cream cheese cubes, and then with the remaining bread cubes. ♦ In a blender container or a mixing bowl with a rotary beater, mix together eggs, milk, melted butter or margarine, and maple syrup till well combined. Pour egg mixture evenly over bread and cheese cubes. Using a spatula, slightly press layers down to moisten. Cover with plastic wrap and refrigerate for 2 to 24 hours. ♦ Remove plastic wrap from baking dish. Bake in a 325° oven for 35 to 40 minutes or till the center appears set and the edges are lightly golden. Let stand about 10 minutes before serving. Serve with the Apple Cider Syrup. Makes 6 to 8 servings.

This Apple Cider Syrup is a wonderful complement to the Stuffed French Toast

Strata on the opposite page.

APPLE CIDER SYRUP
(Pictured on pages 48–49)

½ cup sugar
4 teaspoons cornstarch
½ teaspoon ground cinnamon
1 cup apple cider *or* apple juice
1 tablespoon lemon juice
2 tablespoons butter *or* margarine

In a small saucepan stir together the sugar, cornstarch, and cinnamon. Then stir in the apple cider or juice and lemon juice. ♦ Cook and stir the mixture over medium heat till mixture is thickened and bubbly. Then cook and stir for 2 minutes more. ♦ Remove saucepan from heat and stir in the butter or margarine till melted. Makes about 1⅓ cups.

***E**ditor's Tip: A good cup of coffee adds a finishing touch to a delicious breakfast or brunch. Brewing the perfect cup is simple. ♦ Begin with fresh ground coffee. (To keep ground coffee fresh, store it in an airtight container in the freezer.) ♦ Always use the correct grind for the type of brewing method. Use a coarse grind for percolator brewing, medium grind for drip, and fine grind for espresso. ♦ Make your coffee with freshly drawn cold water. ♦ It's important not to overbrew coffee. Allow no more than 6 to 8 minutes when percolating coffee, 4 to 6 minutes when making drip coffee, and 1 to 3 minutes for espresso.*

Although breakfast is served between 7:30 and 9:30 a.m., guests often linger later,

visiting while enjoying a second cup of coffee.

REFRIGERATED BRAN MUFFINS
(Pictured on pages 48–49)

2½ cups all-purpose flour
2½ teaspoons baking soda
¾ teaspoon salt
3 cups whole bran cereal
1 cup *boiling* water
2 beaten eggs
2 cups buttermilk
1½ cups sugar
½ cup cooking oil
1 cup raisins

In a medium mixing bowl stir together flour, baking soda, and salt. Set flour mixture aside. ♦ In a small mixing bowl place *1 cup* of the bran cereal. Pour the boiling water over the cereal and set aside. ♦ In a large mixing bowl combine eggs, buttermilk, sugar, cooking oil, and the remaining bran cereal. Add flour mixture to egg mixture. Stir just till moistened. Then add the soaked bran and stir just till well combined. Fold in raisins. ♦ Transfer the batter to a covered container and refrigerate it overnight or for up to 3 days. ♦ To bake, grease 2½-inch muffin cups or line muffin cups with paper bake cups. Spoon batter into the prepared cups, filling each ⅔ full. Bake in a 400° oven for 15 to 20 minutes or till tops spring back when lightly touched. Makes about 24 muffins.

The staff of innkeepers gets creative inspiration from looking through magazines

and cookbooks.

ORANGE MUFFINS
(Pictured on pages 48–49)

1 cup raisins *or* dried currants
1 cup sugar
½ cup butter *or* margarine, softened
2 tablespoons dairy sour cream
2 eggs
2 cups all-purpose flour
¼ teaspoon salt
1 teaspoon baking soda
⅔ cup buttermilk
2 teaspoons finely shredded orange peel
1 recipe Orange Glaze

Grease eighteen 2½-inch muffin cups or line them with paper bake cups. Set muffin cups aside. ♦ If using raisins, place them in a food processor bowl. Cover and process raisins till finely chopped. *Or,* use a knife to finely chop raisins. Set raisins aside. ♦ In a medium mixing bowl beat sugar, butter or margarine, and sour cream with an electric mixer on medium to high speed till fluffy. Beat in eggs. ♦ In a small mixing bowl stir together flour and salt. Then add flour mixture to butter mixture, beating on low speed just till combined. ♦ Stir baking soda into buttermilk. Then stir buttermilk mixture into the batter just till combined. Fold in chopped raisins or currants and orange peel. ♦ Spoon batter into the prepared muffin cups, filling each ⅔ full. Bake in a 400° oven for 14 to 15 minutes or till a wooden toothpick inserted near each center comes out clean. *Immediately* brush the hot muffin tops with the Orange Glaze. Makes 18 muffins.
♦ **Orange Glaze:** In a small bowl or dish stir together ⅓ cup *sugar* and ¼ cup *orange juice.* Makes about ⅓ cup.

Afternoon Tea and More

Old-fashioned hospitality

is at its best when you combine good food with good friends.

And what could be more neighborly than to welcome your guests as inns do,

with a special afternoon tea, a casual get-together snack,

or an early evening hors d'oeuvre.

Time seems to turn back almost 200 years as guests drive up the evergreen-lined lane to **The Westerfield House** in Freeburg, Illinois. The hand-built 18th-century log cabin, with its wide-planked floors and antique furnishings, takes guests back to a different time. One of the many highlights at The Westerfield House is innkeeper Jim Westerfield's guided tour through his colonial-style herb garden. The beautiful formal garden is filled with more than 140 types of herbs, including about 40 different varieties of mint. Jim and his wife Marilyn use mint to flavor this old-time lemonade. It is just one of the many recipes featuring fresh herbs that is served at The Westerfield House.

LEMONADE

2½ **cups water**
2 **cups sugar**
¾ **cup loosely packed fresh mint leaves, rinsed and patted dry**
1 **cup lemon juice (about 6 lemons)**
¼ **cup orange juice**
Ice cubes
Fresh mint
Thin lemon slices

For the syrup, in a medium sauce-pan heat water and sugar over medium heat till sugar is dissolved. Then reduce heat to medium-low and cook, uncovered, for 5 minutes. Remove from heat and let cool for 20 to 30 minutes. ♦ In a large bowl place the ¾ cup mint leaves. Stir lemon juice and orange juice into the syrup. Then pour the lemon-orange mixture over the mint in the bowl. Cover and let stand at room temperature for 1 hour. ♦ Strain mint from the lemon-orange mixture. Discard mint. ♦ To serve, for *each* serving, in a large glass stir together ⅔ cup *cold water* and ⅓ cup lemon-orange mixture. Add ice cubes and garnish with additional mint and a lemon slice. Makes 12 to 15 (8-ounce) servings.

♦ **Note:** To make ahead, prepare the lemon-orange mixture as directed above. Store the mixture in a tightly covered container in the refrigerator for up to 1 week. To serve, prepare as above.

Visions of sugar plums come alive during the magical season of Christmas at **The Victorian Villa Inn** in southern Michigan. Each weekend between Thanksgiving and Christmas, innkeepers Ron and Susan Gibson recreate a Victorian Christmas with all of its nostalgic trimmings, foods, and traditions. Christmas at the Villa begins on Friday night with a traditional American-style Victorian dinner followed by a magic show and harpsichord music. Saturday events include a Victorian Christmas tea, a 19th-century tree-ornament workshop, and a seven-course Charles Dickens-style feast featuring roast goose with chestnut stuffing. The evening closes with wassail, caroling, and chestnuts roasting in the fireplace.

ENGLISH COUNTRY WASSAIL
(Pictured on page 60)

1 recipe Baked Apples in Brandy Sauce (see opposite page)
3 medium oranges
2 tablespoons whole cloves
1 gallon (16 cups) apple cider *or* apple juice
1 quart (4 cups) cranberry juice cocktail
2 teaspoons aromatic bitters (optional)
¾ cup sugar
30 inches stick cinnamon
1 tablespoon whole allspice
2 to 2½ cups dark rum (optional)

Prepare Baked Apples in Brandy Sauce as directed. ♦ Meanwhile, stud oranges with cloves, then cut *each* orange into *eight* wedges; set aside. ♦ In an 8-quart Dutch oven stir together apple cider or juice, cranberry juice, and, if desired, aromatic bitters. ♦ Add oranges, sugar, stick cinnamon, and allspice. Bring just to a simmer; reduce heat. Cover and heat for 10 minutes. ♦ If desired, stir in dark rum and heat through. Transfer to large, heat-proof serving bowl. Add baked apples. If desired, stir in the 1 cup reserved brandy sauce from the apples. Makes about 21 (8-ounce) servings.

◆ **Baked Apples in Brandy Sauce:** Core 8 small *apples* (about 2 pounds total). Peel off a strip around the top of each apple. Place the apples in a 13x9x2-inch baking dish; set aside. ◆ For brandy sauce, in a small saucepan combine 1 cup packed *brown sugar*, ½ teaspoon ground *cinnamon*, ¼ teaspoon ground *nutmeg*, and ⅛ teaspoon ground *allspice*. Stir in 1 cup *brandy*. Carefully bring just to boiling over medium-low heat. Pour brandy sauce over apples in dish. Cover with foil and bake in a 350° oven for 25 to 30 minutes or till the apples are just tender when tested with a fork. ◆ Use a slotted spoon to remove the apples from the brandy sauce. If desired, reserve *1 cup* of the brandy sauce for the wassail. *Or,* serve the apples with sauce as a dessert in individual dessert bowls. Makes 8 servings.

English Country Wassail
(see recipe, page 58)

Peppertrees Bed & Breakfast Inn, a unique 1905 home, draws its name from the two large peppertrees stationed in the front yard. The main rooms of this stately, red brick, Victorian house, located two blocks from the University of Arizona campus in Tucson, are furnished with antiques from innkeeper Marjorie Martin's family in England. Through a set of French doors and across a landscaped patio are two guesthouses. Each guesthouse has two bedrooms, a living room, dining area, full kitchen, a washer and dryer, and a private patio. In addition to the homelike atmosphere, Marjorie offers gracious hospitality. For example, upon arriving, guests are welcomed with a beverage. And each afternoon, a tea of shortbread and other cookies is served.

MAPLE AND PECAN COOKIES

1 cup butter
½ cup sugar
1 egg yolk
3 tablespoons maple syrup
½ teaspoon vanilla
½ teaspoon maple flavoring
2 cups all-purpose flour
1¼ cups finely chopped pecans
36 pecan halves

In a mixing bowl beat butter with an electric mixer on medium to high speed till softened. ◆ Add sugar and beat till fluffy. Add egg yolk, maple syrup, vanilla, and maple flavoring; beat till combined. Beat or stir in flour. Stir in chopped pecans. If necessary, cover and chill dough about 1 hour or till easy to handle. ◆ Divide dough in half. Shape each half into a 10-inch roll. Wrap in waxed paper or plastic wrap, and refrigerate for at least 2 hours. ◆ Cut the dough into ½-inch-thick slices. Place slices 2 inches apart on an ungreased cookie sheet. Slightly press a pecan half in the center of each cookie. Bake in a 325° oven about 20 minutes or till lightly golden around edges. Remove the cookies and cool them on a wire rack. Makes 36.

Behind the doors of a large, gray, 1828 home with Federal and Greek Revival features awaits a truly unforgettable afternoon tea at **Sarah's Dream.** The inn, located in the Finger Lakes region of New York state, is run by innkeepers Judi Williams and Ken Morusty. Judi and Ken pay close attention to details. The tables are set to perfection with delicate antique china, heirloom silver, and white, starched linens. Judi personally prepares six homemade items each day and offers 10 different kinds of teas to her guests. Soft background music adds a finishing touch of elegance to their memorable four-course tea parties.

QUICKIE QUICHES

1 recipe Pastry for Single-Crust Pie
3 slightly beaten eggs
⅓ cup milk
¼ cup light cream _or_ half-and-half
¼ teaspoon dried oregano, crushed
⅛ teaspoon white pepper
⅛ teaspoon dried sage leaves, crushed
Dash garlic powder
1 cup shredded sharp cheddar cheese (4 ounces)*
½ cup chopped canned roasted sweet red peppers*

Prepare Pastry for Single-Crust Pie as directed. ◆ On a floured surface, roll pastry to ⅛-inch thickness. For 2½-inch quiches, cut twelve 4-inch circles; for 1¾-inch quiches, cut twenty-four 3-inch circles. Line 2½-inch muffin cups with 4-inch circles or 1¾-inch muffin cups with 3-inch circles; set aside. ◆ In a bowl combine eggs, milk, light cream, oregano, white pepper, sage, and garlic powder. ◆ Sprinkle cheese and red peppers in pastry-lined cups. Pour egg mixture into each cup. Bake in a 350° oven about 15 minutes for 1¾-inch quiches, about 20 minutes for 2½-inch quiches, or till filling appears set. Cool in muffin cups for 10 minutes; remove from cups. ◆ Serve warm. _Or,_ wrap in foil and freeze. Reheat, covered with foil, on a baking sheet in a 325° oven about 25 minutes. Makes 12 (2½-inch) or 24 (1¾-inch) quiches.
◆ *For 1¾-inch quiches, decrease cheddar cheese to _½ cup_ and roasted red peppers to _¼ cup._
◆ **Pastry for Single-Crust Pie:** In a bowl stir together 1¼ cups _all-purpose flour_ and ¼ teaspoon _salt._ Cut in ⅓ cup _shortening_ till pieces are the size of small peas. Sprinkle with 1 tablespoon _cold water,_ then toss with a fork. Repeat with 2 to 3 tablespoons _cold water,_ adding 1 tablespoon at a time, till all is moistened. Form dough into a ball.

Innkeeper Jim Westerfield, of **The Westerfield House** in southwest Illinois, is said to hold the title of "Windsor-Chair Nut of the Midwest." For 35 years, Jim has been collecting these beautiful curved-back chairs. His antique chairs can be found throughout the three-level log cabin inn. Guests are invited to use the chairs as they dine in the Westerfield's colonial dining room, when they write a letter, or even as they sit to tie their shoes.

SEEDED SAGE 'N' CHEDDAR WAFERS

2 tablespoons sesame seed
1½ cups all-purpose flour
3 tablespoons snipped fresh sage
or **1 tablespoon dried sage, crushed**
2 tablespoons poppy seed
¼ to ½ teaspoon ground red pepper
8 ounces white *or* yellow sharp cheddar cheese, cubed
½ cup *cold* butter *or* margarine, sliced into tablespoons

In a medium skillet cook and stir sesame seed over medium-low heat till golden. Transfer toasted sesame seed to a large mixing bowl. ♦ Stir flour, sage, poppy seed, and red pepper into sesame seed in bowl. Set flour mixture aside. ♦ In a food processor bowl place cheese. Cover and process cheese till very fine. Add flour mixture and cold butter or margarine. Cover and process just till mixture *begins* to form a ball. ♦ Transfer dough to a lightly floured surface and shape dough into a 12-inch-long roll. If dough is too soft to slice, wrap it in plastic wrap and chill it in the refrigerator till firm. ♦ Using a sharp knife, cut the dough into ⅛-inch-thick slices. Place dough slices on an ungreased baking sheet. Bake in a 400° oven for 7 to 8 minutes or till edges are golden. Remove from baking sheet and cool on wire racks. Makes about 96.

A 3½-hour drive from Philadelphia or New York City transports travelers to a village that bills itself as "the town time forgot." Eagles Mere, Pennsylvania, nestled in the Endless Mountains, was once a thriving summer resort area that attracted hundreds of affluent urban families at the turn of this century. During this time, magnificent Victorian summer cottages and hotels were built. The first hotel in the area was the Lewis Hotel, now known as the **Eagles Mere Inn.** Today, guests at this three-story, comfortably decorated inn enjoy the relaxing ambience that brought guests here more than 100 years ago. Large, overstuffed chairs in the common room offer peaceful relaxation, and a downstairs pub invites friendly gatherings to play a game of darts or pool. Guests also can enjoy picnics, swimming, fishing, and boating at nearby Eagles Mere Lake. A demanding 18-hole golf course, excellent tennis courts, miles of groomed cross-country ski trails, a pond for skating, and the reknowned Eagles Mere Toboggan Slide are other attractions available to visitors at Eagles Mere Inn.

SHARP PINEAPPLE SPREAD

¼ cup drained canned crushed pineapple
1 3-ounce package cream cheese, softened
1 to 2 teaspoons grated *or* prepared horseradish
Assorted crackers

In a small bowl stir together drained pineapple, cream cheese, and horseradish. Cover and chill for at least 2 hours for flavors to blend. ♦ Serve with assorted crackers. Makes 4 (2-tablespoon) servings of spread.

In southwest Mississippi, near the city of Natchez, is the **Monmouth Plantation,** one of the area's splendid antebellum mansions built during the prosperous 1800s. Meticulously restored to its former grandeur, the Monmouth is situated on 26 acres of lovely landscaped grounds and gardens. This former home of General John A. Quitman, a Mexican War hero, U.S. congressman, and governor, is beautifully decorated with many pieces from his family's household. Today, guests enjoy freshly mixed mint juleps and hors d'oeuvres served in the late afternoon in either the charming courtyard or John Quitman's handsome study.

CAVIAR PIE

6 hard-cooked eggs, chopped
1 medium onion, chopped (½ cup)
or **½ cup sliced green onion**
3 tablespoons mayonnaise
2 3-ounce packages cream cheese
1 8-ounce carton dairy sour cream
1 to 2 2-ounce jars black caviar, well-drained
Lemon twists
Fresh mint
Assorted crackers

In a medium mixing bowl stir together chopped eggs, chopped onion, and mayonnaise. Spread egg mixture in a 9-inch pie plate. ♦ In a small bowl beat cream cheese with an electric mixer till softened. Add sour cream, then beat till combined. Dollop cream cheese mixture by small spoonfuls on top of the egg layer in the pie plate, then spread evenly. Cover with plastic wrap and refrigerate for 2 to 24 hours. ♦ To serve, spoon caviar evenly on top of the cream cheese mixture. Garnish with lemon twists and fresh mint. Serve with assorted crackers. Makes 14 to 16 (¼-cup) servings of spread.

*Hannah Marie Country Inn
in Spencer, Iowa*

Mad Hatter Tea Party

Surrounded by
hundreds of acres of corn and soybeans in
northwest Iowa is the Hannah Marie
Country Inn, a peaceful respite from the
hustle and bustle of modern city life.
Overnight guests at the inn enjoy swinging
in the hammock under the trees, playing
croquet on the lawn, sleeping in beds
covered with Iowa-made quilts,
soaking in a claw-footed bathtub, and
walking along a nearby creek.
Despite all this home-style luxury, food really
is what takes center stage at the Hannah
Marie. Guests can experience one of several
themed teas, such as the one shown here, or
dine on a lunch of French country-style
food. Even breakfasts are special
at the Hannah Marie, because seconds are a
must and desserts are included.

The "queen" of country teas can be found holding court at the Hannah Marie Country Inn, a restored Victorian farmhouse in Spencer, Iowa.

"Queen" Mary Nichols, a former home economics teacher, and her husband, Ray, bought their farmhouse in 1972 with plans to retire there. But when they did retire in 1983, they decided to embark on new careers as innkeepers and turned the farmhouse into a country inn. They named the inn for Mary's mother, who was born and raised about three miles away.

The charming inn is furnished with antiques and curiosities such as turn-of-the-century magazines, a doll collection, old photograph albums, and figurines.

"Hospitality is a happening. When guests arrive, they're expecting a full day of entertainment."

"Hospitality is a happening," says Mary when explaining her philosophy of innkeeping. "When guests arrive, they're expecting a full day of entertainment." What they get is that and more. Mary's themed teas, ranging from Queen Victoria's chocolate tea to tea at the Ritz, welcome both overnight and drop-in guests to a theatrical food experience.

For her Mad Hatter tea party, "Queen" Mary dons a red dress studded with gold hearts. The scene is set by the telling of Lewis Carroll's story, "Alice in Wonderland."

A Mad Hatter, often portrayed by Mary's cousin, Scott Gibson, invites guests to sit down for tea in the dining room where the tables are dressed in pretty, lacy linens and delicate china.

Guests then are treated to a three-course tea featuring foods that are an integral part of the Lewis Carroll story. In the well-loved story, Alice falls down the treacle (molasses) well into Wonderland, so Treacle Tartlets start off the second course of the tea. The fictional Alice nibbles on a small eat-me cake, which makes her grow shorter or taller. At the Hannah Marie tea, guests enjoy Mary's Eat-Me Cakes and Meringue Mushrooms while glancing around the table to see if anyone has grown. And, to celebrate the unbirthday from the storybook, Strawberry Roulade is served with an *un*birthday candle.

If tea parties aren't their cup of tea, guests can enjoy French bistro-style dining at lunchtime. A heartwarming, hearty fare, such as cassoulets, soups, and stews, is featured at Mary's second, and nearby, guesthouse, the Carl Gustav.

"We love innkeeping, even the long hours, the fast scrambles . . . What better place to do this than in northwest Iowa."

"Most of the dishes feature flavors that people are used to—only with a twist to make them a little unusual. It's simple, plain country cooking," Mary says.

To reach the Carl Gustav, which opened in early 1991, guests just need to follow a covered walkway that winds through the garden from the Hannah Marie.

The Carl Gustav, named for Mary's Swedish grandfather, has a relaxed and informal atmosphere. The inn's decor is eclectic with Victorian and European influences.

Mary and Ray have a pact that if innkeeping ever stops being fun, they'll quit. That's unlikely, according to Mary.

"We love innkeeping, even the long hours, the fast scrambles when guests arrive hours early, and the creativeness it takes to stretch the budget. What better place to do this than in northwest Iowa—blue skies, little crime, and uncrowded highways," Mary says.

Mary serves these tasty, open-face sandwiches as

the tea's first course.

TURKEY TEA SANDWICHES

½ **cup whole cranberry sauce**
½ **teaspoon prepared horseradish**
8 very thin slices white *or* **wheat bread (4 to 5 inches in diameter)**
or **whole wheat dinner rolls, split**
½ **cup mayonnaise** *or* **salad dressing**
1 teaspoon snipped dill *or* ¼ **teaspoon dried dillweed**
8 large leaves leaf lettuce
12 ounces thinly sliced, cooked turkey
Grapes *or* **desired potato** *or* **pasta salad (optional)**

In a small mixing bowl stir together cranberry sauce and horseradish. Set cranberry mixture aside. ◆ If using bread slices, trim crusts from the bread. ◆ In another small mixing bowl stir together mayonnaise or salad dressing and dill or dillweed. Spread the mayonnaise mixture on bread slices or split dinner rolls. Place slices or open dinner rolls on small individual plates. ◆ Top each bread slice or roll with a lettuce leaf. Then top with turkey, rippling the slices on top to fit. Spoon the cranberry mixture on top. *Or,* spoon the cranberry mixture in individual paper cups and place a cup on each plate. ◆ If desired, garnish the plates with grapes or desired potato or pasta salad. Makes 8 servings.

The entire family helps with the tea—Mary's son David makes the scones and

her husband, Ray, bakes them.

SCONES
(Pictured on pages 66–67)

2 cups all-purpose flour
4 teaspoons sugar
1 tablespoon baking powder
⅛ teaspoon baking soda
⅔ cup *cold* butter *or* margarine
⅔ cup buttermilk
2 tablespoons buttermilk
Butter
Desired preserves

Lightly grease a baking sheet. Set baking sheet aside. ♦ In a medium mixing bowl stir together flour, sugar, baking powder, and baking soda. Cut in ⅔ cup butter or margarine till mixture resembles coarse crumbs. Make a well in the center of the dry mixture, then add ⅔ cup buttermilk. Use a fork to stir just till moistened. ♦ Turn the dough out onto a lightly floured surface. Quickly knead dough by gently folding and pressing the dough for 10 to 12 strokes or till the dough is *nearly* smooth. Pat or lightly roll the dough to 1-inch thickness. ♦ Cut dough with a floured 2½-inch biscuit cutter, dipping the cutter into flour between cuts. Place scones about 2 inches apart on the prepared baking sheet. Brush tops with the 2 tablespoons buttermilk. Bake in a 400° oven about 15 minutes or till golden. Serve scones hot with the additional butter and preserves. Makes 8 to 10.

The second course can be called the "sweet course." Guests enjoy Treacle Tartlets,

Scones, Eat-Me Cakes, Meringue Mushrooms, and Apple 'n' Juice Sorbet.

TREACLE TARTLETS
(Pictured on pages 66–67)

1 recipe Tart Pastry
½ cup butter *or* margarine, softened
½ cup sugar
2 eggs
1 teaspoon vanilla
¼ cup self-rising flour*
1 tablespoon molasses
Whipped cream (optional)

Prepare Tart Pastry as directed.
♦ On a well-floured surface, roll pastry to a ⅛-inch thickness. Using a 3-inch-round cutter, cut out circles. Then line 2½-inch oval or round fluted tartlet pans with the pastry circles. Place tartlet pans in a 15x10x1-inch baking pan. Cover lightly with plastic wrap and freeze about 30 minutes or till pastry is firm. ♦ Meanwhile, for filling, in a medium mixing bowl beat butter or margarine and sugar with an electric mixer on medium to high speed till light and fluffy. Add eggs and vanilla; beat just till combined. Add self-rising flour; beat on *low speed* just till combined (mixture will appear curdled). ♦ In a custard cup stir together molasses and 1 teaspoon *water*. Lightly brush insides of frozen pastry shells with the molasses mixture. ♦ Spoon filling into the pastry shells, filling each to ¼ inch from the top. Bake in a 350° oven for 15 to 20 minutes or till tops are lightly golden and filling appears set. Remove tartlets from pans and cool on a wire rack. If desired, use a decorating bag fitted with a large tip to pipe whipped cream on top of tartlets just before serving. Serve the same day. Makes about 14.
♦ *You may substitute ¼ cup *all-purpose flour*, ¼ teaspoon *baking powder*, and a dash *salt* for the ¼ cup self-rising flour.
♦ **Tart Pastry:** In a food processor bowl place 1 cup *all-purpose flour* and 2 tablespoons *sugar*. Cover and process till mixed. Add ½ cup very cold *butter* or *margarine*, cut up. Cover; process till pieces are the size of coarse crumbs. Add 1 *egg*; cover and process just till mixture *begins* to form a ball. Press into a ball. Cover and chill till easy to handle.

As they bite into these little cakes, children's eyes grow big in anticipation of

becoming taller or shorter.

EAT-ME CAKES
(Pictured on pages 66–67)

½ **cup sugar**
2 egg yolks
½ **cup unsalted butter, melted**
1 teaspoon finely shredded lemon peel
1 tablespoon lemon juice
½ **cup self-rising flour***
2 slightly beaten egg whites
Powdered sugar (optional)

Grease and flour twenty-four 3-inch madeleine molds; set aside. ♦ In a medium mixing bowl beat sugar and egg yolks with an electric mixer on medium to high speed about 30 seconds or till thoroughly mixed. Add melted butter, lemon peel, and lemon juice. Beat on low speed till combined. ♦ Sift or sprinkle *one-fourth* of the self-rising flour over the egg-yolk mixture. Gently fold in the flour. Fold in the remaining flour by fourths. Stir in the slightly beaten egg whites till combined. ♦ Spoon batter into the prepared molds, filling each about half full. Bake in a 375° oven for 10 to 12 minutes or till edges are golden and tops spring back when lightly touched. Cool cakes in molds for 1 minute. Use a knife to loosen cakes from molds; invert cakes onto wire racks to cool. If desired, just before serving, sift powdered sugar over the cake tops. Makes 24.
♦ *You may substitute ½ cup *all-purpose flour*, ½ teaspoon *baking powder*, ¼ teaspoon *salt*, and ⅛ teaspoon *baking soda* for the ½ cup self-rising flour.
♦ **Note:** To make ahead, prepare, bake, and cool cakes as directed above. Place them in a covered airtight container and store at room temperature for up to 1 day or in the freezer for up to 6 months. To serve, thaw if frozen. If desired, sift powdered sugar over cake tops.

These sweet little mushrooms are oh-so good and oh-so easy to make.

MERINGUE MUSHROOMS
(Pictured on pages 66–67)

4 egg whites
1 cup sugar
2 teaspoons unsweetened cocoa powder
¼ cup desired jam *or* preserves

Lightly butter and flour a baking sheet. Set baking sheet aside. ♦ In a large mixing bowl beat egg whites with an electric mixer on medium speed till soft peaks form (tips curl). Gradually add *½ cup* of the sugar, 1 tablespoon at a time, beating on high speed till very stiff peaks form (tips stand straight). Sprinkle the remaining sugar on top, then gently fold in. ♦ Spoon meringue mixture into a decorating bag fitted with a large plain-round tip (about a ½-inch opening). ♦ On the prepared baking sheet, make the mushroom tops separate from the mushroom stems. For the mushroom tops, pipe rounded mounds of meringue about 1¼ to 1½ inches in diameter. For the mushroom stems, pipe straight mounds about ⅝ inch tall. Use a wet knife to cut meringue stems from the pastry tip. ♦ Lightly sift cocoa powder over mushroom tops. Bake meringues in a 300° oven for 25 to 30 minutes or till slightly dry and crisp. Carefully transfer meringues from baking sheet to wire racks to cool. ♦ To assemble, attach stems to tops by gently twisting a stem into the bottom of each mushroom top to make a slight indentation. Use a small amount of jam to stick the mushroom tops and stems together. Makes about 40.
♦ **Note:** To make ahead, prepare, bake, and cool mushroom tops and stems as directed above, but *do not assemble.* Place tops and stems in a covered airtight container. Store at room temperature for 2 or 3 days or for up to 2 weeks in the freezer. To serve, uncover and let stand at room temperature about 30 minutes. Then assemble as above.

Mary suggests that if you want to serve the sorbet on the same plate as the second

course, spoon it into a paper cup and place the cup away from the hot scone.

APPLE 'N' JUICE SORBET
(Pictured on pages 66–67)

2¼ **cups water**
⅓ **cup sugar**
1 15- *or* 16-ounce can *or* jar applesauce
1 12-ounce can frozen apple-orange-pineapple juice
concentrate, thawed

In a large pitcher or mixing bowl stir together the water and sugar till sugar is dissolved. Stir in the applesauce and juice concentrate. ♦ Pour the apple mixture into a 4-quart ice cream freezer. Freeze apple mixture according to manufacturer's directions. ♦ To serve the sorbet, scoop it into small paper cups or dishes. Makes 1½ quarts.

*E**ditor's Tip:** The comforting ritual*

of afternoon tea is kept alive by many innkeepers. As a relaxing way

to entertain in your own home, start celebrating

this delightful custom. It can be just a simple occasion with a pot of piping hot

tea and scones, or an elaborate affair that includes

an array of sweet and savory treats. ♦ A traditional tea begins at 4 o'clock

or thereabouts. Set the table with your finest china

and linen or lace tablecloth and napkins. Limit tableware to tea cups, saucers,

dessert plates, spoons, and forks. ♦ Foods should be kept to the

size of one or two bites. A traditional teatime fare includes a variety of cookies,

pastries, biscuits, cakes, and finger sandwiches.

Everyone gets to blow out a candle at this "unbirthday" celebration. Mary suggests

dimming the lights before serving this final course.

STRAWBERRY ROULADE
(Pictured on pages 66–67)

1 recipe Sponge Cake
Powdered sugar
4 cups strawberries, quartered
2 tablespoons sugar
¾ cup strawberry preserves
2 tablespoons cherry brandy
Whipped cream (optional) ♦ 10 small candles

Prepare and bake Sponge Cake. When cake is done, *immediately* loosen it from pan. Invert cake onto a towel sprinkled with powdered sugar. Roll up warm cake and towel, jelly-roll style, starting from one of the short sides. Cool completely. ♦ Meanwhile, in a medium mixing bowl lightly toss strawberries and sugar; cover and chill. ♦ Stir together strawberry preserves and brandy. When cake is cool, gently unroll cake. Spread preserve mixture on cake to within ½ inch of edges. Roll up cake *without* towel, jelly-roll style, starting from one of the short sides. ♦ To serve, cut the cake roll into 1-inch-thick slices. Place slices on plates. Spoon strawberries and their syrup on top. If desired, top each with whipped cream. Add a candle, light it, and serve. Makes 10 servings.

♦ **Sponge Cake:** Grease and flour a 15x10x1-inch baking pan; set aside. In a small bowl stir together ¼ cup sifted *cake flour* and 2 tablespoons *cornstarch;* set aside. ♦ In a medium bowl beat 3 *egg yolks,* 1 *whole egg,* ⅓ cup *sugar,* and ½ teaspoon *vanilla* with an electric mixer on high speed about 5 minutes or till thick and lemon-colored. ♦ Wash and dry beaters. In another mixing bowl beat 2 *egg whites* and ⅛ teaspoon *cream of tartar* till soft peaks form (tips curl). Add 1 tablespoon *sugar,* then beat till stiff peaks form (tips stand straight). ♦ Fold egg yolk mixture into egg white mixture. Sprinkle flour mixture over egg mixture; gently fold in just till combined. Spread batter evenly in the prepared pan. Bake in a 450° oven about 5 minutes or till cake springs back when lightly touched. Makes 1 cake.

Five-Star Dining

*L*ike people, each inn has its own

unique personality, which in the case of an inn, is defined by the decor,

amenities, and, of course, the selection of fine food that it serves. In this chapter,

you'll find wonderful appetizers, entrées, side dishes, and desserts that reveal

the individual charms of each inn.

There's no place like home during Christmastime, unless you're a holiday guest at the **Old Rittenhouse Inn.** On the two weekends before Christmas in Bayfield, Wisconsin, innkeepers and former music teachers Jerry and Mary Phillips present wassail dinner concerts in their Queen Anne-style mansion. While guests dine on splendid food, local singers and instrumentalists dressed in period costumes perform Christmas carols and holiday music. The warm hospitality, cheery holiday-decorated rooms, and generous holiday spirit make Christmas at the Old Rittenhouse Inn a time to remember.

CRANBERRY CONSOMMÉ

1 16-ounce package frozen unsweetened sliced rhubarb
2 cups water
½ cup sugar
3 inches stick cinnamon
2 cups cranberry juice
½ cup burgundy
½ cup carbonated water
Fresh mint (optional)

In a medium saucepan combine rhubarb, water, sugar, and cinnamon. Bring to boiling. Reduce heat and simmer, uncovered, for 5 minutes or till rhubarb is tender. Remove from heat and discard stick cinnamon from mixture. Pour rhubarb mixture into a strainer and press out the juice. (You should have about *2¼ cups* rhubarb juice.) ♦ Stir cranberry juice and wine into rhubarb juice. If desired, chill juice mixture till serving time. ♦ To serve, in a saucepan heat juice mixture just till warm. Gently stir in carbonated water. Ladle into consommé cups or small bowls. If desired, garnish with fresh mint. Serve warm. Makes 8 (⅔-cup) servings.

Good, basic food with an emphasis on freshness makes dining a pleasurable experience at the **Eagles Mere Inn** in Eagles Mere, Pennsylvania. Each evening, a six-course dinner is served by candlelight in the Victorian-decorated dining room of this 15-guest-room inn. Innkeeper Joan Fiocchi oversees the meal preparations, making sure only the finest, freshest ingredients are used. All breads, desserts, and soups are homemade. This delicious Roquefort-Vegetable Soup, served as a second course, has become a favorite with her guests.

ROQUEFORT-VEGETABLE SOUP

¼ cup butter *or* margarine
4 cups chopped cabbage
3 cups chopped cauliflower
3 cups chicken broth
1 cup whipping cream
¼ cup crumbled Roquefort cheese (1 ounce)
Croutons
Salt
Coarsely ground pepper

In a 3-quart saucepan melt butter or margarine. Stir in cabbage till well coated. Cook, uncovered, over low heat for 10 to 15 minutes or till cabbage is soft, stirring occasionally. ◆ Stir cauliflower and chicken broth into cabbage mixture. Bring to boiling over high heat. Then reduce heat. Cover and simmer about 30 minutes or till cabbage and cauliflower are tender. ◆ Stir cream and Roquefort cheese into vegetable mixture. Heat through. ◆ To serve, ladle into small bowls. Garnish with croutons. Serve with salt and pepper so each person can season to taste. Makes 6 (1-cup) servings.

Hillbrook Inn, an English manor-style cottage sitting on 17 acres of landscaped gardens, looks and feels like a country home in Europe. Innkeeper Gretchen Carroll, who has traveled in England, France, and Germany, brings a sense of European hospitality to the countryside of West Virginia.

A stay at Hillbrook combines elegance with comfort. Guests are able to take pleasure in priceless art without feeling as though they're in a museum, and can enjoy an intimate, candlelight, gourmet dinner without wearing a coat and tie. This combination of elegance and informality is a rare delight and brings guests back to Hillbrook again and again.

CREAM OF FENNEL SOUP

¼ cup unsalted butter
1½ to 2 cups chopped fresh fennel (about 1 pound without tops *or* 2 small bulbs)
½ cup chopped onion
1 cup homemade *or* canned chicken broth
¼ cup whipping cream
1 tablespoon Pernod *or* desired anise liqueur
⅛ teaspoon coarsely ground black pepper
Crème fraîche *or* dairy sour cream
Fennel leaves

In a 2-quart saucepan melt butter. Stir in fennel and onion till well coated. Cover and cook over low heat for 20 to 25 minutes or till very tender, stirring occasionally. ♦ In a blender container or food processor bowl place fennel mixture and *¼ cup* of the chicken broth. Cover and blend or process till smooth; return to the saucepan. Add remaining chicken broth, cream, Pernod, and pepper. If desired, heat or chill. ♦ Serve either warm or chilled. To serve, ladle into small bowls. Garnish each with crème fraîche or sour cream and a leaf of fennel. Makes 4 (⅔-cup) servings.

It's a lobster fantasy come true at **The Blue Hill Inn** located in the coastal village of Blue Hill, Maine. By request, the inn prepares a tantalizing "Lobster Fantasy" dinner in which three courses feature fresh Maine lobster. The creative menu includes a lobster bisque glazed with cognac cream, Lobster 'n' Wild Rice Salad, and a lobster ragout. The 150-year-old, Federal-style inn also is well known for its other candlelight, six-course dinners that showcase local seafood, native-raised lamb, and produce from local growers. Dinner at this intimate and comfortable inn is certainly an experience to be savored.

LOBSTER 'N' WILD RICE SALAD

20 asparagus spears (1 pound)
⅔ cup wild rice
2 oranges
1 tablespoon white wine vinegar
½ cup walnut oil
1 medium carrot, finely chopped
½ cup coarsely chopped walnuts
1 shallot, finely chopped
2 tablespoons snipped fresh mint
8 cooked lobster claws *or* 8 ounces cooked lobster meat, cut into large pieces

To prepare asparagus, wash and scrape off scales. Break off woody bases. Cook asparagus, covered, in a small amount of boiling *salted water* for 8 to 10 minutes or till nearly tender. Drain, cover, and chill. ♦ To cook wild rice, rinse rice well. In a saucepan bring 1⅔ cups *water* to boiling. Add rice. Cover and simmer about 40 minutes or till tender. If necessary, drain rice; cool to room temperature. ♦ Meanwhile, finely shred enough peel from the oranges to make *1 tablespoon;* set aside. Section oranges over a bowl to catch juices. (You should have about *1 tablespoon* juice.) Cut orange segments in half; set aside. ♦ For dressing, add vinegar and ⅛ teaspoon *salt* to orange juice in bowl. Using a wire whisk, very slowly whisk in walnut oil till well mixed. ♦ To arrange salads, on *each* dinner plate alternately arrange *five* asparagus spears and *five* or *six* orange half-sections in spoke fashion. Spoon wild rice in center. Drizzle with some dressing. Combine orange peel, carrot, walnuts, shallot, mint, and *1 tablespoon* of the dressing. Sprinkle carrot mixture on top of rice. Then arrange lobster on top and drizzle with remaining dressing. Makes 4 appetizer servings.

Pella, meaning a "city of refuge," was just that to immigrants from Holland who came to central Iowa in the mid-1800s seeking new freedoms. Today, visitors come to Pella, Iowa, seeking a city with old-world charm. The town square, with its Dutch architecture, klokkenspel (or glockenspiel) and flowering courtyard, resembles a charming, picturesque village in the Netherlands. Located just a few blocks away from the town square is the **Strawtown Inn.**

Operating in a 130-year-old home, this inn fills the senses with Dutch spirit. Rooms are warmed by the delft-tiled fireplaces and decorated with Dutch furnishings, lace curtains, and Hindeloopen folk painting. Authentic Dutch meals of Blinden Vinken (stuffed veal rolls), gekruid rundvlees (Dutch spiced beef), and Hollandse frits (Dutch fried potatoes) are brought to the table by servers in Dutch outfits. Their warm and inviting hospitality adds to the many splendors of the past found at Pella's Strawtown Inn.

BLINDEN VINKEN

1¼ **pounds boneless veal leg round steak, cut ½ inch thick**
2 **slightly beaten eggs**
1 **rusk, finely crumbled (about 3 tablespoons)**
2 **teaspoons finely chopped onion**
2 **teaspoons very finely snipped fresh parsley**
½ **teaspoon ground nutmeg**
¼ **teaspoon salt**
⅛ **teaspoon pepper**
8 **ounces ground beef** *or* **ground veal,** *or* **a mixture of ground pork** *plus* **beef** *or* **veal**
1 **tablespoon shortening** *or* **cooking oil**
⅓ **cup low-sodium chicken broth** *or* **beef broth**
1 **recipe Mushroom Sauce**

Cut veal steak into *four* portions. Place each piece between 2 pieces of heavy plastic wrap. Lightly pound each piece with a meat mallet to form a rectangle about ¼ inch thick; set veal aside. ♦ For stuffing, in a bowl stir together eggs, crumbled rusk, onion, parsley, nutmeg, salt, and pepper. Add ground meat and mix well. Divide stuffing into *four* portions. Form each portion into a cylinder shape; place *one* on top of *each* veal piece. Roll veal around stuffing. Tie each roll with string. ♦ In a large skillet heat shortening or oil. Cook veal rolls on all sides about 5 minutes or till well browned. Drain veal rolls on paper towels, then place them in an 8x8x2-inch baking dish. ♦ Discard fat from skillet. Pour broth into the skillet and heat, scraping bottom of skillet well to loosen all particles. Pour heated broth over veal rolls in baking dish. Cover with foil. Bake in a 325° oven about 40 minutes or till veal is tender and ground meat is no longer pink. Serve with Mushroom Sauce. Makes 4 servings.

♦ **Mushroom Sauce:** In a small saucepan cook 1½ cups sliced fresh *mushrooms* and 2 teaspoons finely chopped *onion* in 2 tablespoons *butter* or *margarine* about 3 minutes or till vegetables are tender. Stir in ½ teaspoon *lemon juice*. ♦ In a small bowl combine ¾ cup low-sodium *chicken* or *beef broth*, 3 tablespoons dry *red wine*, 4 teaspoons dry *oxtail soup mix*, and 1 tablespoon *all-purpose flour*. ♦ Stir broth mixture into vegetable mixture. Cook and stir till thickened and bubbly. Cook and stir for 1 minute more. Makes about 1⅓ cups.

In Ashland, Oregon, just two blocks away from the world-famous Oregon Shakespeare Festival, is a majestic Victorian home known as **The Winchester Country Inn.** The charming Queen Anne-style inn blends sophistication with comfort. Upstairs in this 1886 home are seven gracious guest rooms decorated with Victorian pieces. A glassed-in dining room and an outdoor patio overlooking the English gardens and gazebo provide lovely dinner settings. For dining pleasure, The Winchester Country Inn offers a cosmopolitan cuisine that innovatively combines flavors from many countries.

TENG DAH FILLET

1 3-pound beef tenderloin
2 tablespoons finely shredded lemon peel
1 teaspoon cracked black pepper
½ cup soy sauce
⅓ cup lemon juice
2 tablespoons sugar
1 tablespoon prepared horseradish
4 cloves garlic, minced, *or* 2 teaspoons bottled minced garlic
2 teaspoons ground black pepper
⅛ teaspoon aniseed, crushed
⅛ teaspoon ground cinnamon
Dash ground nutmeg
Wasabi paste (Japanese horseradish)(optional)

Use a sharp boning knife to carefully remove most of the fat and silver skin from the tenderloin. ♦ Use a paring knife to make small ½-inch-deep cuts about 1 inch apart down the length of the tenderloin. Then stuff a small amount of the lemon peel and cracked pepper into each pocket. Place the tenderloin in a plastic bag set in a shallow baking dish; set aside. ♦ For marinade, in a medium mixing bowl stir together ½ cup *water,* soy sauce, lemon juice, sugar, prepared horseradish, garlic, ground black pepper, aniseed, cinnamon, and nutmeg. Pour marinade over tenderloin in the bag. Close bag; marinate meat in the refrigerator for 4 to 24 hours, turning bag occasionally. ♦ Remove meat from bag; reserve marinade. Place meat on a rack in a shallow roasting pan. Add ¼ *cup* of the marinade to the pan. Roast in a 425° oven about 1 hour for rare doneness. Meanwhile, in a saucepan bring remaining marinade to boiling; strain. ♦ To serve, slice meat across grain. Spoon heated marinade on top of meat. If desired, serve with a small amount of Wasabi paste. Serves 6 to 8.

At the **Liberty Hall Inn** in Pendleton, South Carolina, four-course dinners are served by candlelight in either the garden room or the larger Hunt Room. Each dining area has a personality of its own. The garden room, with its vaulted ceiling, tall windows, French doors, fresh flowers, and dusty pink shades, provides a light, graceful setting. The Hunt Room, with its forest green carpet, beadboard paneling, horse paintings, and brass accents, inspires a cozier dining atmosphere. Meals at the Liberty Hall Inn are uncomplicated and generous. The daily dinner menu includes the house specialty, Marinated Beef Tenderloin, three or four other entrées, soup, salad, and dessert. At the Liberty Hall Inn, comfortable surroundings and delicious food combine for dining at its best.

MARINATED BEEF TENDERLOIN

½ **cup ruby port wine**
¼ **cup olive oil**
¼ **cup soy sauce**
½ **teaspoon dried thyme, crushed**
¼ **teaspoon bottled hot pepper sauce**
1 **bay leaf**
4 **beef tenderloin steaks, cut 1 to 1¼ inches thick (6 to 8 ounces each)**

In a medium bowl stir together wine, olive oil, soy sauce, thyme, ½ teaspoon *pepper*, ¼ teaspoon *salt*, hot pepper sauce, and bay leaf. ♦ Place beef in a plastic bag set in a large bowl. Pour wine mixture over meat. Close bag and marinate beef in the refrigerator for 3 to 6 hours, turning the bag occasionally. ♦ Line a 13x9x2-inch baking pan with foil, then place a rack in the pan. Remove beef from bag and discard the marinade. Place beef on the rack in the foil-lined pan. Bake in a 450° oven for 8 minutes. Turn beef over and bake for 8 to 10 minutes more for rare doneness. Makes 4 servings.

In the heart of Oak Creek Canyon in Arizona, travelers can stop at **Garland's Oak Creek Lodge** for a comfortable place to stay and a home-cooked meal prepared by chef Amanda Stine. While at the lodge, guests can choose from a variety of relaxing activities. They can play tennis or walk through the lodge's fruit orchards, drop a fishing line into Oak Creek or a nearby trout lake, or visit the many boutiques and art galleries in Sedona. Or, if they choose, guests can just pull up a chair on the porch of their rustic cabin and take it easy.

BEEF FILLETS WITH RED CHILI SAUCE

½ **of 1 dried** *or* **canned Chipotle chili pepper, seeds and stem removed***
2 cups beef broth
½ **cup chopped sweet red pepper**
¼ **cup chopped onion**
3 dried mild New Mexico red chili peppers, seeds and stems removed*
4 cloves garlic, minced, *or* **2 teaspoons bottled minced garlic**
1 cup whipping cream
4 *or* **6 beef tenderloin steaks, cut 1 to 1¼ inches thick (about 6 ounces each)**

If using a *canned* Chipotle chili pepper, rinse it under cold water; drain. ♦ In a medium saucepan stir together Chipotle chili, broth, sweet red pepper, onion, mild chili peppers, and garlic. Bring to boiling; reduce heat. Cover; simmer about 1 hour or till peppers are very tender. (Mixture will be reduced to about *1¾ cups.*) Slightly cool mixture. ♦ In a blender container or food processor bowl place *half* of the mixture. Cover and blend or process till nearly smooth. Strain mixture through a sieve, pressing well. Discard solids. Repeat with remaining chili mixture. ♦ Transfer mixture to the saucepan. Stir in cream; bring to boiling. Reduce heat. Gently boil, uncovered, about 30 minutes or till reduced to about *1 cup,* stirring occasionally. ♦ Meanwhile, to cook steaks, place steaks on the unheated rack of a broiler pan. Broil 3 inches from heat 13 to 17 minutes for medium doneness. ♦ Serve sauce with steaks. Makes 4 or 6 servings.
♦ *Because chili peppers contain volatile oils that can burn skin and eyes, avoid direct contact with peppers as much as possible. Wear plastic or rubber gloves or work under cold running water. If your bare hands touch the peppers, wash your hands and nails well with soap and water.

Grilled Lamb with Honey-Mustard Sauce
(see recipe, page 92)

For an evening of casual elegance, artful cuisine, and warm hospitality, visit the **Hotel Carter** located 300 miles north of San Francisco. In a bright, airy dining room filled with contemporary art and pine furnishings, innkeepers Mark and Christi Carter serve innovative, romantic dinners. They try to use only the finest, freshest ingredients to create masterpieces that please both the palate and the eye. Dinner consists of an appetizer, between-course sorbet, soup, a choice of two entrées, and a selection of the hotel's award-winning pastries. The Hotel Carter, built in 1986, is a replica of a 19th-century hotel. It combines the charm and graciousness of a country inn with the services and amenities one would expect from a modern hotel.

GRILLED LAMB WITH HONEY-MUSTARD SAUCE
(Pictured on page 91)

2 8-rib lamb rib roasts (about 2 pounds each)*
¼ teaspoon salt
¼ teaspoon pepper
¼ cup snipped fresh sage
¼ cup snipped fresh rosemary
¼ cup snipped fresh thyme
2 tablespoons snipped fresh parsley
⅓ cup lemon juice
1 recipe Honey-Mustard Sauce (see opposite page)

Trim excess fat from top of rib roasts. Then trim and scrape the top and sides of each rib so 1 to 2 inches of each rib bone is completely exposed. ♦ Sprinkle roasts with salt and pepper. ♦ In a small bowl combine sage, rosemary, thyme, and parsley. If desired, remove *2 tablespoons* of the herb mixture and set aside for garnish. Sprinkle remaining herb mixture on the roasts, patting mixture on the roasts to coat well. ♦ *To grill meat,* in a covered grill arrange *medium* coals around a foil drip pan. Test for *medium-low* heat above the pan by placing your hand above the drip pan. You should be able to hold your hand there for 5 seconds. Place roasts, meaty sides up, on the grill rack over the drip pan but not over the coals. (If necessary, to make the meat fit on the rack, tilt the roasts so that their rib bones interlock.) Insert a meat thermometer. Lower grill hood. Grill for 50 to

60 minutes or till thermometer registers 150°, basting occasionally with lemon juice. ♦ Or, *to roast meat,* place roasts, meaty sides up, in a shallow roasting pan. Insert a meat thermometer. Roast, uncovered, in a 325° oven for 45 to 60 minutes or till thermometer registers 150°, basting occasionally with lemon juice. ♦ To serve, cut roasts between rib bones into chops. Spoon the Honey-Mustard Sauce onto each warm dinner plate and arrange 2 chops in a fanned position on top of the sauce. If desired, sprinkle with the reserved herb mixture. Serves 8.

♦ *For easier carving, have the butcher loosen the back bones from the lamb rib roasts.

♦ **Honey-Mustard Sauce:** In a 10-inch skillet stir together 1 cup *dry white wine;* 3 to 4 *shallots,* chopped (3 to 4 tablespoons); and 3 cloves *garlic,* minced. Cook, uncovered, over high heat for 10 to 15 minutes or till mixture is reduced to *2 tablespoons.* ♦ Stir in 3 cups *whipping cream.* Bring to boiling, then reduce heat. Gently boil, uncovered, for 10 to 15 minutes or till mixture is thickened and reduced to *2 cups.* Cool slightly. ♦ In a blender container or food processor bowl place the mixture. Add 3 tablespoons *Dijon-style mustard,* 2 tablespoons *honey,* ¼ teaspoon *salt,* and ⅛ teaspoon *white pepper.* Cover and blend or process till smooth. Strain through a fine sieve. Makes about 2¼ cups.

In New Castle, Delaware, visitors are able to relive a bit of America's colonial past. New Castle was Delaware's first capital and much of its historic heritage has been preserved. The town has many attractions for visitors, including five museums offering glimpses of life during the Dutch and English colonial periods, the Market Place where the public has traded since 1682, and examples of architecture from the early 1700s to 1800s.

Located in the center of the historic district is **The David Finney Inn.** Built in 1685, the inn has been completely restored and is decorated with antiques and period reproductions. The inn has 13 guest rooms, four suites, and a courtyard overlooking formal gardens.

PORK TENDERLOIN WITH PLUM SAUCE

1 12-ounce pork tenderloin
2 plums, pitted and sliced (about 8 ounces total)
⅓ cup port wine
3 tablespoons water
2 to 3 teaspoons finely snipped fresh rosemary
½ teaspoon sugar
⅛ teaspoon salt
1 tablespoon water
1½ teaspoons cornstarch

To cook the meat, place the tenderloin on a rack in a shallow roasting pan. Insert a meat thermometer. Roast, uncovered, in a 425° oven for 25 to 35 minutes or till the thermometer registers 160° to 170°. ♦ Meanwhile, in a medium saucepan combine sliced plums, port wine, the 3 tablespoons water, rosemary, sugar, and salt. Bring to boiling, then reduce heat. Cover and simmer for 3 minutes. Stir together the 1 tablespoon water and cornstarch, then stir cornstarch mixture into plum mixture. Cook and stir till thickened and bubbly. Then cook and stir for 2 minutes more. ♦ To serve, bias-slice the pork tenderloin. Spoon sauce, but not the plums, on a serving platter. Alternately arrange pork slices and plum slices on top of the sauce. Makes 2 or 3 servings.

On a hillside overlooking the West River Valley in southern Vermont is **Windham Hill Inn**, a blissful vision of a New England country inn. The carefully restored 1825 farmhouse, with its white clapboard siding and turn-of-the-century barn, sits on 160 wooded acres. The secluded inn has 15 guest rooms—10 in the main inn and five in the barn. Each room is comfortably furnished with restored country antiques and painted in soft colors. In addition to the homey ambience, friendly hospitality, and fine service from innkeepers Ken and Linda Busteed, the exceptional food at Windham Hill completes the picture of what a New England inn should be.

PORK TENDERLOIN WITH MAPLE-MUSTARD SAUCE

½ teaspoon ground nutmeg
½ teaspoon dried thyme, crushed
¼ teaspoon salt
¼ teaspoon dried basil, crushed
¼ teaspoon ground red pepper
¼ teaspoon ground cloves
¼ teaspoon ground cinnamon
¼ teaspoon ground black pepper
⅛ teaspoon ground allspice
¾- to 1-pound pork tenderloin
3 bay leaves
2 tablespoons olive oil
1 recipe Maple-Mustard Sauce

In a custard cup or small dish stir together nutmeg, thyme, salt, basil, red pepper, cloves, cinnamon, black pepper, and allspice. Sprinkle spice mixture over the pork tenderloin and rub it in with your fingers. Place bay leaves along bottom of tenderloin. Wrap in plastic wrap and refrigerate for at least 2 hours. ◆ To cook the meat, place the tenderloin on a rack in a shallow roasting pan. Brush tenderloin with olive oil. Insert a meat thermometer. Roast, uncovered, in a 425° oven for 25 to 35 minutes or till the thermometer registers 160° to 170°. ◆ To serve, discard bay leaves. Bias-slice the pork tenderloin and serve with the Maple-Mustard Sauce. Serves 4.
◆ **Maple-Mustard Sauce:** In a small mixing bowl use a wire whisk to stir together ⅓ cup pure *maple syrup* and 2 tablespoons *Dijon-style mustard* till smooth. Serve sauce at room temperature. Makes about ½ cup.

Innkeeping in the southern tradition seemed like the perfect answer to Tom and Susan Jonas' search for a new career. Tom, a 17-year veteran of the advertising business, always wanted to own his own business. And Susan, who is from Kentucky, longed to live in the South again. These factors, combined with their love of old houses, antiques, and entertaining, lured them into purchasing the **Liberty Hall Inn** in Pendleton, South Carolina, in 1987. The inn, a former plantation house tucked away in the northwest corner of the state, sits on four acres of meadow and forest. The setting, along with the inn's two open, wrap-around porches for rocking or swinging, creates a haven from daily pressures and makes the perfect place for Tom and Susan to enjoy their new life.

CHICKEN FLORENTINE

4 12-ounce whole chicken breasts
½ cup ricotta cheese
¼ cup grated Parmesan cheese
¼ cup shredded mozzarella cheese (1 ounce)
1 10-ounce package frozen chopped spinach, thawed and
well drained
1 tablespoon butter *or* margarine, melted
1 cup Marinara Sauce

Skin and bone chicken breasts, but *do not split breasts in half.* Place each piece between 2 pieces of plastic wrap. Lightly pound to ¼-inch thickness. ♦ On half of the boned side of *each* chicken breast, spread *2 tablespoons* ricotta cheese; sprinkle with *1 tablespoon* Parmesan cheese and *1 tablespoon* mozzarella cheese. Top with *one-fourth* of the spinach. Fold chicken in half to cover filling. ♦ Arrange in a 13x9x2-inch baking dish. Brush with butter. Bake in a 350° oven for 20 to 25 minutes or till chicken is no longer pink. ♦ To serve, transfer to plates; top *each* breast with ¼ *cup* Marinara Sauce. Serves 4.
♦ **Marinara Sauce:** In a medium saucepan cook ¼ cup chopped *onion* and 2 cloves *garlic,* minced, *or* 1 teaspoon bottled minced *garlic* in 2 tablespoons hot *olive oil* about 5 minutes or till tender. Stir in one 16-ounce can *undrained tomatoes,* cut up; one 6-ounce can *tomato paste;* 1 tablespoon *sugar;* 1 teaspoon dried *basil,* crushed, *or* 1 tablespoon snipped fresh *basil;* ½ teaspoon *salt;* and ⅛ teaspoon dried *oregano,* crushed, *or* ½ teaspoon snipped fresh *oregano.* Bring to boiling, then reduce heat. Cover and simmer for 30 minutes. Store unused sauce in a covered container in the refrigerator for up to 1 week or in the freezer for up to 3 months. Makes 2½ cups.

When the dinner bell rings at **Lone Mountain Ranch** in Big Sky, Montana, guests look forward to a well-balanced, casual, gourmet meal prepared by chef Neil Navratil. Neil tantalizes their palates with both barbecue and international dishes.

A typical dinner at Lone Mountain Ranch includes a choice of four entrées, a salad of crisp greens, a vegetable, freshly baked bread, and a homemade dessert.

CRAB 'N' CILANTRO STUFFED CHICKEN BREASTS

¼ cup all-purpose flour
1 3-ounce package cream cheese, softened
2 tablespoons sliced green onion
1 to 2 tablespoons snipped fresh cilantro
4 ounces flaked, cooked crabmeat (¾ cup)
4 8-ounce whole chicken breasts, skinned and boned
1 tablespoon cooking oil
1 recipe Hot Peanut Sauce

For flour mixture, in a pie plate stir together flour, ⅛ teaspoon *salt,* and ⅛ teaspoon *pepper.* Set flour mixture aside. ♦ For filling, in a small bowl stir together cream cheese, green onion, cilantro, ⅛ teaspoon *salt,* and ⅛ teaspoon *pepper.* Then stir in crabmeat. Set filling aside. ♦ Place each chicken breast between 2 pieces of plastic wrap. Lightly pound to ¼-inch thickness. ♦ On half of the boned side of *each* chicken breast, spread *2 tablespoons* of filling. Fold chicken in half to cover filling. Roll chicken breast in flour mixture till coated. ♦ In a large skillet heat oil over medium heat. Cook chicken breasts about 5 minutes or till golden brown, turning once. Reduce heat to medium-low and cook, uncovered, for 10 to 15 minutes more or till chicken is tender and no longer pink, turning once. ♦ To serve, transfer chicken to dinner plates and spoon Hot Peanut Sauce over each chicken breast. Makes 4 servings.
♦ **Hot Peanut Sauce:** In a blender container or food processor bowl place ½ cup *peanuts.* Cover and blend or process till finely ground; set aside. ♦ In a small saucepan cook 2 tablespoons finely chopped *onion;* 1 small clove *garlic,* minced; and ⅛ teaspoon grated *gingerroot* in 1 tablespoon *cooking oil* over medium-low heat till tender. Stir in ground peanuts, ¼ teaspoon *sesame oil,* and dash ground *red pepper* till smooth. Then add ½ cup *chicken broth,* about 2 tablespoons at a time, stirring till smooth after each addition. Heat through. Makes ¾ cup.

The search for a better recipe is never ending at **The Inn at Honey Run** in Millersburg, Ohio. Innkeeper Marjorie Stock and her staff take great pride in providing their guests with only the very best. All the food is made from scratch and freshness is emphasized. In winter months, the inn holds Thursday Tastings. For these special events, guests are invited to serve as members of a taste panel where they evaluate recipes in side-by-side tastings. To appear on the menu, an item must receive at least a 7 on a 10-point scale.

Perfection also can be found in the accommodations. Built in 1982, the contemporary structure of glass, cedar, and stone is nestled on 60 acres of woods and pasture. All 36 rooms have comfy, upholstered chairs and lamps for reading; tables for writing or game playing; and concealed televisions. Some rooms also have wood-burning fireplaces, and bathtubs with whirlpool jets. Superb food, comfort, serenity, and friendliness are "in" at this inn.

BONELESS BREAST OF COUNTRY CHICKEN

4 boneless skinless chicken breast halves (about 1 pound total)
½ teaspoon dried marjoram *or* basil, crushed
¼ teaspoon salt
¼ teaspoon pepper
⅔ cup light cream *or* half-and-half
2 tablespoons margarine *or* butter, melted
½ cup fine dry bread crumbs
4 orange twists

Place each chicken piece, boned side up, between 2 pieces of plastic wrap. Working from the center to the edges of the chicken, lightly pound with a meat mallet to ½-inch thickness. ♦ Place chicken in a single layer in an 11x7x1½-inch baking dish. Sprinkle with marjoram or basil, salt, and pepper. Then pour light cream or half-and-half over chicken. Cover with plastic wrap and marinate in the refrigerator for at least 4 hours or overnight, turning once. ♦ Remove chicken from marinade. Discard marinade. Use paper towels to pat chicken slightly dry. ♦ Brush chicken with melted margarine or butter. Then roll chicken in the bread crumbs till coated. ♦ Place chicken on the unheated rack of a broiler pan. Broil 4 to 5 inches from the heat for 5 minutes. Turn chicken over and broil for 5 to 7 minutes more or till chicken is no longer pink and coating is golden brown and crispy. ♦ To serve, transfer chicken to dinner plates and garnish with orange twists. Makes 4 servings.

A couple's dream for a romantic getaway becomes reality at the **Hotel Manisses.** Built in 1872 on Rhode Island's Block Island, the hotel reflects the gracious past of the Victorian era. The 18-guest-room hotel is decorated with turn-of-the-century furniture. Guests are able to relax in the hotel's romantic parlors, sipping tea in the afternoon or an after-dinner beverage in the evening. For dinner, guests can choose to dine in the main dining room at candle-lit tables, in the glass-enclosed Garden Terrace dining room, or outdoors under umbrella-topped tables overlooking a beautiful rock garden and fountain.

TUNA WITH RED PEPPER COULIS

2 sweet red peppers
1 tablespoon olive oil
3 cloves garlic, peeled
¾ cup fish broth *or* fish bouillon
3 tablespoons crème fraîche *or* dairy sour cream
Dash salt
Dash white pepper
1 recipe Basil Tuna Steaks

To roast red peppers, cut peppers lengthwise in half. Remove stems and seeds; rinse. Brush skins with olive oil. Place peppers, skin sides up, on a baking sheet. Bake in a 425° oven for 10 minutes. Add garlic cloves to baking sheet; bake about 10 minutes more or till red-pepper skins are charred. ◆ *Immediately* place peppers only in a paper bag; fold bag. Let stand till cooled. ◆ When peppers are cool, peel and discard skins. In a blender container or food processor bowl place the peppers and garlic. Cover; blend or process till smooth. ◆ Transfer mixture to a saucepan. Stir in fish broth. Bring to boiling. Simmer about 5 minutes or till mixture is reduced to *1⅓ cups.* Use a wire whisk to stir in crème fraîche, salt, and pepper. ◆ To serve, place fish on plates; spoon red pepper coulis around fish. Serves 4.
◆ **Basil Tuna Steaks:** Brush 4 *tuna, halibut,* or *swordfish steaks,* cut about 1 inch thick (about 2 pounds total), with 2 tablespoons *olive oil.* Sprinkle with 2 tablespoons snipped fresh *basil.* Cover; wrap in plastic wrap. Chill 1 hour. ◆ *To grill fish,* place fish on a grill rack. Grill fish on an uncovered grill directly over *medium-hot* coals for 4 to 6 minutes per ½-inch thickness or till fish flakes, turning once. ◆ Or, *to broil fish,* place fish on the unheated rack of a broiler pan. Broil 4 inches from heat for 4 to 6 minutes per ½-inch thickness or till fish flakes, turning once. Serves 4.

The goal of the **San Juan Guest Ranch** in southwestern Colorado is to provide guests with the best vacation they'll ever have. When visiting this ranch, even a novice rider feels like a pro after receiving pointers from the ranch's trained wranglers. The wranglers make sure that everyone knows how to ride safely and properly. In addition to the comprehensive riding program, the staff offers friendly, personal service and nine comfortable guest rooms for an at-home feeling. To top off a visit to the San Juan Guest Ranch, good wholesome food is served that satisfies even the hungriest of guests.

HOMEMADE HIRTENSILAT

1 3-ounce package cream cheese
½ of a small cucumber, halved lengthwise and thinly sliced (1 cup)
1 tomato, cut into chunks (1 cup)
1 small onion, thinly sliced and separated into rings (½ cup)
1 small sweet red *or* green pepper, cut into thin strips,
***or* ½ cup sweet red *and* green pepper strips**
½ cup pitted ripe olives
1 recipe Hirtensilat Dressing
Lettuce leaves

Place cream cheese in the freezer about 15 minutes or till very firm but not frozen. ♦ Meanwhile, in a medium bowl combine cucumber, tomato, onion rings, sweet pepper strips, and olives. Drizzle Hirtensilat Dressing over salad, and lightly toss till coated. ♦ Cut cream cheese into small cubes. Add cream cheese to salad, then lightly toss. ♦ To serve, transfer salad to a lettuce-lined medium salad bowl or spoon onto lettuce-lined salad plates. Serves 4.
♦ **Hirtensilat Dressing:** In a screw-top jar combine 2 tablespoons *olive oil*, 1 tablespoon snipped fresh *parsley*, 1 tablespoon *red wine vinegar*, 1 teaspoon *Dijon-style mustard*, ⅛ teaspoon *sugar*, ⅛ teaspoon *onion salt*, ⅛ teaspoon *garlic salt*, ⅛ teaspoon *paprika*, and ⅛ teaspoon *pepper*. Cover and shake well. Makes ¼ cup.

The friendliness of a country inn, plus the service of professional conference planning, offers business travelers a unique package. This package can be found at **The Inn at Honey Run,** which is located in the heart of Ohio's Amish country, midway between Cleveland and Columbus. It's perfect for a corporate retreat. To accommodate business clientele, the inn has everything from meeting rooms with the latest audiovisual equipment to 36 guest rooms for housing a large group. In their free time, corporate guests are able to unwind in the inn's exercise rooms, hike through the woods on wildflower trails, or just curl up in front of the fireplace with a good book or magazine.

FRESH BROCCOLI SLAW

1½ **cups finely chopped broccoli flowerets**
1 **cup peeled and finely chopped broccoli stems**
1 **small tomato, seeded and chopped (½ cup)**
¼ **cup finely chopped green pepper**
1 **tablespoon chopped green onion**
¼ **teaspoon salt**
1 **recipe Creamy French Dressing**
6 **tomato wedges**
6 **fresh parsley sprigs**

In a medium mixing bowl combine broccoli flowerets, chopped broccoli stems, chopped tomato, green pepper, and green onion. Sprinkle salt over broccoli mixture, then drizzle with French dressing. Toss till well coated. Cover and chill. ♦ To serve, spoon broccoli mixture into small bowls or saucers. Garnish each serving with a tomato wedge and parsley sprig. Serves 6.
♦ **Creamy French Dressing:** In a small mixing bowl use a wire whisk to stir together ¼ cup *mayonnaise* or *salad dressing,* 2 tablespoons *sugar,* 1 tablespoon *cider vinegar,* 1 tablespoon *catsup,* 1 tablespoon *salad oil,* 1 teaspoon prepared *mustard,* 1 teaspoon *lemon juice,* ⅛ teaspoon *salt,* ⅛ teaspoon *paprika,* dash *garlic powder,* and dash bottled *hot pepper sauce* till thoroughly mixed. Makes ½ cup.

In 1972, innkeepers Brooks and Joyce Kaufman purchased a 1750 stone barn next door to their home and turned it into a charming country inn with five antique-filled guest rooms and three dining rooms. The decor and menu at **The Inn at Phillips Mill,** located in New Hope, Pennsylvania, are basically country French. Entrées such as fillet of beef with béarnaise sauce, salmon with watercress sauce, and steak au poivre are complemented at each meal with as many as four or five locally grown vegetables.

PUREED SWEET POTATOES

4 medium carrots, cut up
2 large sweet potatoes, peeled and quartered (1 pound total)
¼ cup butter, softened
¼ teaspoon salt
⅛ teaspoon pepper
3 to 4 tablespoons whipping cream, light cream, *or* half-and-half

In a large covered saucepan cook carrots for 10 minutes in enough *boiling water* to cover. Add sweet potatoes. Return to boiling. Cover and cook about 30 minutes or till vegetables are very tender. Drain. ♦ Transfer cooked carrots and sweet potatoes to a large mixing bowl and beat with an electric mixer till smooth. Add butter, salt, and pepper. Beat till combined. Then beat in enough cream or half-and-half till moistened. ♦ If necessary, return to saucepan and heat through over low heat, stirring occasionally. *Or,* transfer to a 1-quart casserole. Cover and chill for 2 to 24 hours. To serve, bake, covered, in a 350° oven about 45 minutes or till heated through. Makes 6 servings.

On warm summer days in Maine, guests are encouraged to relax and enjoy one of the **Penobscot Meadows Inn's** popular homemade ice creams while overlooking Penobscot Bay. Innkeepers Dini and Bernie Chapnick renovated this turn-of-the-century Victorian home in 1984.

They masterfully combined comfort with sophistication. Throughout the inn, there are weavings, hand-made quilts, and country antiques for a cozy, homey feeling. Yet the food at this inn is quite elegant. Dini and Bernie tantalize their guests with champagne lobster, veal scampi, triple-chocolate terrine, and these rich ice creams.

PENOBSCOT MEADOWS' HOMEMADE ICE CREAMS

2 quarts (8 cups) whipping cream
2 cups sugar
8 egg yolks

For ice cream base, in a large sauce-pan bring *1 quart* of the cream *almost* to boiling. ♦ Meanwhile, in a large mixing bowl beat together remaining cream, sugar, and egg yolks just till combined. ♦ Gradually stir about *half* of the hot cream into the cold cream mixture. Return cream mixture to the saucepan. Cook and stir for 8 to 10 minutes or till mixture coats a metal spoon. ♦ Cool thoroughly either in an ice-water bath or overnight in the refrigerator. Use the ice cream base for the Apricot-Amaretto Surprise or Chocolate Ice Cream recipes. Makes about 2 quarts (18 servings).

♦ **Apricot-Amaretto Surprise Ice Cream:** Prepare base as above and chill overnight in refrigerator. In a bowl pour ¼ cup *amaretto* over ½ cup chopped dried *apricots;* cover and let stand overnight. ♦ To the chilled base, stir in the soaked apricots and amaretto, ½ cup flaked *coconut,* ½ cup chopped *walnuts,* ½ cup chopped *cranberries,* and ½ cup chopped *semisweet chocolate* or miniature *semisweet chocolate pieces.* Freeze in a 4- or 5-quart ice-cream freezer according to manufacturer's directions. ♦ For a harder ice cream, transfer to a covered container and freeze 24 hours.

♦ **Chocolate Ice Cream:** Prepare base as above, *except* stir in 2 ounces melted *bittersweet* or *semisweet chocolate* and ¾ cup unsweetened *cocoa powder* into the hot, cooked mixture. Then cool base as above. ♦ To the chilled base, stir in ¼ cup *crème de cacao.* Freeze in a 4- or 5-quart ice-cream freezer according to manufacturer's directions. ♦ For a harder ice cream, transfer to a covered container and freeze 24 hours.

In Arlington, the quiet little southwestern Vermont village that inspired painter Norman Rockwell, is a picturesque country inn called **The Arlington Inn.** This 1848 mansion is one of Vermont's finest Greek Revival homes. The 13-guest-room inn has been fully restored to capture the charm and elegance of the mid-19th century. Innkeepers Paul and Madeline Kruzel invite guests to come, relax, and enjoy one of their award-winning gourmet dishes.

SUMMER FRUITS WITH DEVONSHIRE CREAM

½ **cup dairy sour cream**
¼ **cup packed light brown sugar**
3 **tablespoons amaretto** *or* **milk**
½ **cup whipping cream**
1½ **cups cantaloupe balls (about ½ of a medium cantaloupe)**
1 **cup small strawberries**
½ **cup blueberries**
½ **cup blackberries**
½ **cup raspberries**
Fresh mint
Lady fingers *or* **almond cookies (amaretti)**

For the cream topping, in a medium bowl stir together sour cream, brown sugar, and amaretto or milk till smooth. In a small mixing bowl whip whipping cream till soft peaks form. Fold the whipped cream into the sour cream mixture. ◆ In another medium bowl combine cantaloupe balls, strawberries, blueberries, blackberries, and raspberries. ◆ To serve, spoon fruit into large martini glasses or small dessert bowls. Top each with the cream topping. Garnish with mint and cookies. Makes 4 servings.

Innkeeper Nancy Jaspers' love of sweets, baking, and socializing started the **Spring Side Inn's** tradition of an evening dessert hour. Each evening, the long walnut dining table of this 140-year-old Gothic Revival home, located 20 miles south of Dubuque, Iowa, is set with navy placemats, clear glass plates, water goblets, coffee cups, and antique silver flatware. Guests are served such delicacies as these Poached Pears with Grand Marnier Sauce, walnut lace cookies, carrot cake, or chocolate mousse. The evening tradition has become a favorite among the guests as a delightful way to end the day and become acquainted with the other guests.

POACHED PEARS WITH GRAND MARNIER SAUCE

(Also pictured on the cover)

4 ripe medium pears
3 cups water
1¼ cups sugar
2 beaten egg yolks
2 tablespoons water
2 tablespoons Grand Marnier
½ cup whipping cream
Fresh mint ◆ Raspberries (optional) ◆ Melted chocolate (optional)

Peel pears, leaving stems on. Then core pears from blossom ends. ◆ To poach pears, in a medium saucepan bring the 3 cups water and *1 cup* of the sugar to boiling. Carefully add pears, stem ends up. Reduce heat. Cover and simmer about 20 minutes or till pears are tender. Remove saucepan from heat and let pears cool in liquid. ◆ Meanwhile, for sauce, in the top of a double boiler thoroughly combine egg yolks, 2 tablespoons water, and the remaining ¼ cup sugar. Place the top of the double boiler over, but not touching, gently boiling water. Beat with an electric mixer on medium speed about 10 minutes or till mixture is very thick, fluffy, and pale yellow. Remove from heat; transfer to a small bowl. *Immediately* stir in Grand Marnier. Let cool about 10 minutes. ◆ Meanwhile, wash beaters. In another small mixing bowl beat whipping cream till stiff peaks form. Fold whipped cream into egg yolk mixture. ◆ To serve, remove pears from liquid and drain well. Spoon some of the sauce onto dessert plates. Place pears on top of the sauce, then spoon remaining sauce over pears. Garnish with mint and, if desired, raspberries and melted chocolate. Makes 4 servings.

In 1812, the **Buxton Inn** welcomed stagecoach guests who were traveling between Worthington and Zanesville, Ohio. Today, this inn continues to welcome overnight guests who are seeking a quiet getaway. In 1972, innkeepers Orville and Audrey Orr undertook the extensive project of restoring the 19th-century building to its lovely original state. Now, the exterior of the inn appears much as it did when the first stage-coach travelers visited. The interior is painted with warm colors and papered with old-fashioned wall coverings. The furnishings are from the Empire, Victorian, and Federal periods. As one of Ohio's oldest continuously operating inns, the Buxton Inn offers a rich architectural heritage and an old-time ambience to its overnight and dining guests.

HOT WALNUT FUDGE CAKE À LA MODE

1¼ **cups butter *or* margarine**
6 squares (6 ounces) semisweet chocolate
2½ **cups sugar**
6 beaten eggs
3 cups all-purpose flour
½ **cup chopped walnuts**
Ice cream
Chocolate ice-cream topping

In a heavy medium saucepan heat butter or margarine and semisweet chocolate over low heat just till melted, stirring occasionally. Cool slightly. ♦ Stir in sugar and eggs. Then by hand, *lightly* beat in the flour just till combined. ♦ Spread batter into a 15x10x1-inch baking pan. Sprinkle walnuts on top. ♦ Bake in a 350° oven for 20 to 25 minutes or till a wooden toothpick inserted near the center comes out clean. *Do not overbake.* ♦ To serve, cut into squares and serve warm with a small scoop of ice cream and chocolate topping. Makes 24 servings.

The enjoyment and success of owning a Victorian bed-and-breakfast in northern California spurred innkeepers Mark and Christi Carter to build a second inn, called the **Hotel Carter,** across the street. Christi supervises the small restaurant in this exquisite, 20-guest-room hotel. The food is outstanding and features Christi's pastries as one of the many specialties.

TOASTED ALMOND TORTE

1½ **cups sifted cake flour**
1 **teaspoon baking powder**
8 **ounces almond paste, crumbled**
1 **cup sugar**
¾ **cup unsalted butter, softened**
4 **eggs**
¼ **cup toasted almonds, finely ground**
1 **teaspoon vanilla**
1 **to 2 tablespoons powdered sugar**
1 **recipe Grand Marnier Crème à l'Anglaise**
1 **cup whipping cream, whipped**
2 **cups raspberries ◆ Edible lavenders (optional)**

Lightly grease the bottom of a 9-inch springform pan; line with parchment paper. Grease and flour paper and sides of pan. ◆ Sift cake flour and baking powder together. ◆ In a bowl beat almond paste, sugar, and butter till well combined. Beat in eggs, one at a time. Stir in almonds and vanilla. Fold in flour mixture. ◆ Pour batter into the prepared pan. Bake in a 350° oven for 45 to 50 minutes or till a wooden toothpick inserted near the center comes out clean. Cool 10 minutes. Remove torte from pan; cool completely. ◆ To serve, sift powdered sugar on top; cut into wedges. Spoon about ¼ cup Grand Marnier Crème à l'Anglaise onto each dessert plate; top with torte slice. Dollop with whipped cream. Garnish with raspberries and, if desired, lavenders. Makes 12 servings.

◆ **Grand Marnier Crème à l'Anglaise:** In a medium saucepan bring 2 cups whipping cream and 1 vanilla bean, split lengthwise in half, just to boiling, stirring frequently. ◆ In a bowl beat 4 egg yolks and ¾ cup sugar together with an electric mixer for 2 to 3 minutes or till thick and lemon-colored. Gradually stir in about 1 cup of the hot mixture. Return entire mixture to the saucepan. Cook and stir just till mixture returns to boiling; remove from heat. Remove vanilla bean. Stir in 2 to 3 tablespoons Grand Marnier. Cover. Cool; chill in refrigerator. Makes 3½ cups.

When author Sir Arthur Conan Doyle introduced Sherlock Holmes in 1887, little did he know Holmes would be snooping around at **The Victorian Villa Inn** in Union City, Michigan, years later. The 19th-century inn offers Sherlock Holmes' Mystery Weekends for guests who are zealous about solving mysteries and for those who are just looking for a fun getaway. Along with sniffing out clues, guests enjoy a weekend of 19th-century-style meals featuring items such as a roast boar loin entrée, cock-a-leekie porridge soup, and this English Red Raspberry Trifle.

ENGLISH RED RASPBERRY TRIFLE

¾ **cup sugar**
3 **tablespoons cornstarch**
¼ **teaspoon salt**
2¼ **cups milk**
3 **beaten egg yolks**
3 **tablespoons butter** *or* **margarine**
2 **teaspoons vanilla**
1 10¾-**ounce frozen loaf pound cake, thawed**
¼ **cup red raspberry preserves**
⅓ **cup cream sherry**
8 **to** 10 **soft macaroons, crumbled (**2 **cups)**
1 **cup broken pecans**
1 **cup whipping cream, whipped**
Crumbled macaroons
Broken pecans
Red raspberries

For pudding, in a heavy medium saucepan stir together sugar, cornstarch, and salt. Stir in milk. Cook and stir over medium heat till thickened and bubbly. Cook and stir for 2 minutes more. Remove from heat. Gradually stir about *1 cup* of the hot mixture into egg yolks. Return all to the mixture in saucepan. Bring to a gentle boil; reduce heat. Cook and stir for 2 minutes more. Remove from heat. Stir in butter or margarine and vanilla till butter melts. Cover surface with plastic wrap. Cool. ◆ Meanwhile, use a sharp knife to cut the cake horizontally into *three* even layers. Spread *2 tablespoons* of the preserves on the top sides of *each* of the bottom and middle layers.

Reassemble the 3 layers of cake. Then cut the cake crosswise into ⅜-inch slices (about 18 slices). ◆ To assemble trifle, arrange *twelve* slices in the bottom and up the sides of a 2-quart, straight-sided, clear glass serving bowl (cake will not completely cover sides of bowl). Sprinkle with *half* of the sherry. Then sprinkle with *1 cup* of the crumbled macaroons and the 1 cup pecans. Spoon *half* of the pudding on top. Spread *half* of the whipped cream on top of the pudding. Top with remaining cake slices, sherry, 1 cup crumbled macaroons, and pudding. ◆ Sprinkle with additional crumbled macaroons and broken pecans. Use a decorating bag fitted with a large tip to pipe the remaining whipped cream on top of trifle. *Or,* decoratively dollop the remaining whipped cream on top. ◆ Cover and refrigerate for 2 to 24 hours. Garnish with fresh raspberries. Makes 8 to 10 servings.

Once the home of the world-renowned Menninger Clinic, the **Heritage House Historic Inn** in Topeka, Kansas, was transformed into an elegant inn and gourmet restaurant in the late 1980s. Each of the 14 guest rooms in this 1925 farm home has been individually decorated by different local designers. The decor of the rooms ranges from contemporary to period and from formal to country casual. To enter the sunny dining room for lunch or dinner, guests walk through a European-style kitchen and are able to catch a glimpse of the luscious desserts displayed on a table.

AMARETTO CHEESECAKE

15 chocolate sandwich cookies with white filling, broken
1 cup blanched whole almonds
⅓ cup sugar
¼ cup butter *or* margarine, softened
3 8-ounce packages cream cheese, softened
1 cup sugar
4 eggs
½ cup amaretto
⅓ cup whipping cream
1 teaspoon vanilla
1 16-ounce carton dairy sour cream
1 tablespoon sugar
1 teaspoon vanilla
¼ cup toasted sliced almonds *or*
1 cup toasted blanched whole almonds

For crust, in a food processor bowl place cookies, 1 cup whole almonds, ⅓ cup sugar, and butter. Cover and process till fine crumbs form. Press mixture onto the bottom and about 1¾ inches up the sides of a 9-inch springform pan; set aside. ♦ In a large bowl beat cream cheese and 1 cup sugar with an electric mixer till smooth. Add eggs. Beat on low speed just till combined. Stir in amaretto, whipping cream, and 1 teaspoon vanilla. Pour filling into the crust-lined springform pan. ♦ Bake cheesecake on a shallow baking pan in a 375° oven for 40 minutes. Stir together sour cream, 1 table-spoon sugar, and 1 teaspoon vanilla. Carefully spread sour cream mixture on top of the cheesecake. Return cheesecake to 375° oven and bake for 5 minutes more. ♦ Cool in pan for 15 minutes. Loosen crust from sides of pan. Cool 30 minutes more. Remove sides of pan; cool for 4 hours. Cover and refrigerate till serving time. ♦ To serve, garnish with ¼ cup sliced almonds or 1 cup whole almonds. Serves 12 to 16.

At 7 p.m. each evening, guests at **Windham Hill Inn** are invited to a charming dinner party hosted by innkeepers Ken and Linda Busteed. In their homey, 19th-century Vermont farmhouse, Ken and Linda set the scene by playing soft music during dinner and using their best china and table linens. Guests can choose to dine in either the formal dining room at a large, mahogany, Queen Anne table or in a more intimate dining room at small oak tables. The dinner-party menu features a multicourse gourmet meal prepared by Linda. At Windham Hill, dinner is more than a meal—it's an enchanting affair.

LEMON IMPERIAL

¾ **cup all-purpose flour**
¼ **cup finely chopped walnuts**
¼ **teaspoon salt**
6 **tablespoons unsalted butter**
1 8-ounce **package cream cheese, softened**
¾ **cup sifted powdered sugar**
⅔ **cup sugar**
5 **teaspoons cornstarch**
¾ **cup water**
2 **beaten egg yolks**
1½ **teaspoons finely shredded lemon peel**
2 **tablespoons lemon juice**
Desired berries (such as strawberries, blueberries, *and* raspberries)

For crust, in a medium mixing bowl stir together flour, walnuts, and salt. Using a pastry blender, cut in butter till mixture resembles coarse crumbs. Press crumb mixture onto the bottom of an ungreased 8x8x2-inch baking pan. Bake in a 375° oven about 20 minutes or till lightly browned. Cool crust. ♦ For filling, in a small mixing bowl beat cream cheese and powdered sugar together till well combined. Then spread cream cheese mixture over cooled crust. ♦ For topping, in a medium saucepan stir together sugar and cornstarch. Stir in water, beaten egg yolks, lemon peel, and lemon juice. Cook and stir mixture till thickened and bubbly. Then cook and stir for 2 minutes more. Spoon lemon mixture evenly over top of cream cheese layer. Cover and chill about 1 hour or till firm. ♦ To serve, cut into rectangles or squares and top with berries. Makes 8 or 9 servings.

An old-fashioned southern meal awaits guests each evening in the formal dining room of **Madewood,** a home on a former sugar plantation about 40 miles west of New Orleans.

Guests dine on Cajun favorites such as crawfish etoufée, chicken and andouille gumbo, corn bread, greens, and Bread Pudding Supreme with Whiskey Sauce. In the morning, guests are awakened with chicory-flavored coffee delivered to their rooms. And for breakfast, they return to the antique-filled dining room for a hearty meal of grits, ham, eggs, breads, and fruits.

BREAD PUDDING SUPREME

**1 1-pound loaf unsliced French *or* firm-textured bread,
cut into 1-inch cubes (12 cups)
3 cups milk
½ cup butter, softened
1 cup sugar
4 egg yolks
1 teaspoon vanilla
1 large baking apple, peeled, cored, and thinly cut
into round slices
4 egg whites
½ cup sugar
1 recipe Whiskey Sauce**

Grease an 8x8x2-inch baking dish; set aside. ♦ In a large bowl combine bread cubes and milk; let stand 5 minutes. ♦ In another large bowl beat butter and 1 cup sugar with an electric mixer till fluffy. Beat in egg yolks and vanilla. Stir in bread mixture. ♦ To assemble, in the prepared baking dish layer *one-third* bread mixture, *half* of the apple, *one-third* more bread mixture, and then remaining apple. Top with remaining bread mixture. ♦ Place baking dish in a larger baking pan; set pan on oven rack. Pour *hottest tap water* into the larger baking pan to a depth of 1 inch. Bake in a 350° oven 45 minutes or till center appears set. ♦ Meanwhile, for meringue, beat egg whites till soft peaks form (tips curl). Add the ½ cup sugar, *1 tablespoon* at a time, beating on high speed till stiff peaks form (tips stand straight). ♦ Remove pudding from pan of water. Spread meringue over *hot* pudding, sealing meringue to edges of dish. Return baking dish to oven; bake about 15 minutes or till golden. Serve warm with sauce. Serves 8. ♦ **Whiskey Sauce:** In a saucepan combine 1 beaten *egg*, 1 cup *sugar*, and ¼ cup *butter*. Cook and stir just till thickened and mixture begins to boil. Remove from heat. Carefully stir in 2 tablespoons *bourbon*. Slowly stir in ¾ cup *whipping cream*. Slightly cool before serving. Makes 1⅔ cups.

*A roaring campfire at Busterback Ranch
in Ketchum, Idaho*

Trail-Ride Dinner

Nestled among
mountain peaks in an uncrowded valley of the
Sawtooth National Recreation Area in
Idaho is the Busterback Ranch. This ranch
offers the fun of hiking, biking, water sports,
and horseback riding during the summer
and cross-country skiing in winter.
When not busy with these activities, guests
can enjoy delicious, western, family-style meals
served after scenic trail rides. This
menu is just a sampling of the bounty found
at a Busterback trail-ride dinner. Besides
the ranch's great outdoor western barbecue and
Dutch-oven cooking, guests also can dine at
the White Cloud Lodge, where they are
treated to other Busterback specialties such
as baked trout, grilled salmon, and grilled
red chili-spiced pork tenderloin.

117

At the Busterback Ranch in Ketchum, Idaho, guests get a real taste of the American West. The ranch not only offers numerous recreational opportunities, it also gives visitors a chance to see a working ranch with 1,200 head of cattle.

The ranch is a serene haven from the hustle and bustle of workaday living. Overnight guests have their choice of restful retreats, all of which combine old-west warmth with today's conveniences. One choice is an individual log cabin. These cabins feature rough-hewn pine beds and rustic wood stoves as well as electric heat for comfort. Or, guests can settle into a cozy

Kevin's menus use ingredients indigenous to Idaho, such as trout, salmon, beef, and lamb.

private room in the White Cloud Lodge.

When New Yorker Kevin O'Donnell joined the Busterback staff as managing director in 1989, he set out to develop menus geared for the upscale tastes and palates of the ranch's guests, who come from all over the country. Kevin's menus are influenced by both European and western cuisines, and use ingredients indigenous to Idaho, such as trout, salmon, beef, and lamb.

Guests start off the day with a hearty country breakfast served family-style in the Busterback Ranch kitchen. They help themselves to coffee and sample the homemade pastries and other menu items, which may range from eggs and home fries to granola and spiced yogurt. On some days, guests may opt for a brisk morning ride on horseback and a stop for breakfast along the trail.

Later, guests grab a bite of lunch at the lodge or pick up a lunch to go. The menus change with the season. In the winter, lunch may be piping-hot soup and a sandwich, and in the summer, it may be a fresh fruit salad.

At dinnertime, guests have the choice of dining in- or outdoors. Indoors, diners gather around long pine tables in the lodge's dining room for a family-style dinner. During the day, the focal point of the lofty dining room is the spectacular view afforded by the expansive windows. At 7,200 feet above sea level, the

light combined with the clean, crisp air make the dramatic scenery of the Sawtooth and White Cloud mountains sparkle. But when darkness comes, the dining room's imposing fireplace, which is made from polished stones gathered from a nearby mountain river, becomes the center of attention with its cheery light and warmth.

If guests prefer to eat outdoors, they can dine on the lodge's deck or experience a cowboy-led trail ride to a dinner and bonfire afterward.

What's for dinner? Barbecued or grilled specialties, of course. But the real hallmark of Busterback's western cuisine is Dutch-oven cooking. Although the Dutch oven, a covered cast-iron kettle, isn't used for every meal at Busterback Ranch, it is an important tool in the Busterback kitchen and is a must for the trail-ride dinners.

"Cooking food in the Dutch oven—that's the real, traditional West," says Kevin. "I've seen cowboys leaning over their campfire with their cowboy coffee and their Dutch oven, making dinner, whether it be pork and beans or whatever. I learned how to use the Dutch oven from old-timers. You can do everything in a Dutch oven. Because it gets extremely hot, meats turn out great in it, as well as desserts, soups, and breads."

To prove his point, Kevin offers guests the chance to try delicacies such as wild elk prepared in the Dutch oven, as well as old-fashioned favorites including Dutch-oven Idaho potatoes and Dutch-oven apple crisp.

With such terrific dishes to choose from and beautiful scenery to enjoy, it's no wonder guests keep coming back to the Busterback Ranch time and again.

"Cooking food in the Dutch oven—that's the real, traditional West."

rimp in a large ceramic bowl and serves it

ocktail sauce to his guests.

-EAT SHRIMP

can (1½ cups) beer
ay seasoning *or* seasoned salt
small shrimp in shells
cktail sauce

In a large saucepan bring beer and
boiling. Add shrimp. Return to boiling,
overed, for 1 to 3 minutes or till shrimp
. Drain and chill. ◆ Serve with cocktail
ervings.

E*ditor's Tip:* Part of the fun and
excitement of the trail-ride dinner at Busterback Ranch is eating a delicious
dinner in the great outdoors. You, too, can enjoy eating this wonderful meal on a
picnic at the park or at the beach. To ensure your dinner is fresh and safe,
keep these hints in mind. ◆ Before packing the cooler, make sure all of the food is
well chilled. ◆ Use ice packs or blocks of ice in the cooler because they last
longer than ice cubes. ◆ To prepare the Cheesy Potatoes outdoors, pack the onion,
sweet peppers, and cheese in plastic bags. Slice the potatoes at home
and place them in a tightly covered container. Cover the potatoes with water so
they don't turn brown. ◆ Finally, urge everyone to bring along
a hearty appetite to eliminate leftovers.

Kevin, a culinary-school graduate, offers guests inventive and creative foods,

such as this unique tossed salad.

GAZPACHO SALAD
(Pictured on pages 116–117)

1 large cucumber, quartered lengthwise and sliced (2 cups)
3 medium tomatoes, coarsely chopped (2 cups)
1½ cups shredded Monterey Jack cheese (6 ounces)
1 small sweet yellow pepper, cut into thin strips (¾ cup)
1 small sweet red pepper, cut into thin strips (¾ cup)
1 small sweet green pepper, cut into thin strips (¾ cup)
2 2.25-ounce cans sliced pitted ripe olives, drained (optional)
1 recipe Cilantro-Lime Dressing
2 cups tortilla chips, crushed (optional)

In a large salad bowl combine cucumber; tomatoes; cheese; yellow, red, and green peppers; and, if desired, olives. If desired, cover and chill for up to 1 hour. ◆ Drizzle the Cilantro-Lime Dressing over the vegetable mixture. Toss till well coated. If desired, garnish with crushed tortilla chips. Makes 6 to 8 servings.
◆ **Cilantro-Lime Dressing:** In a screw-top jar combine ⅓ cup *salad oil;* 2 tablespoons *lime juice;* 1 tablespoon finely chopped *onion;* 1 tablespoon finely chopped *cilantro;* 1 large clove *garlic,* minced; ¼ teaspoon *salt;* ¼ teaspoon ground *red pepper;* ¼ teaspoon ground *cumin;* and dash *pepper.* Cover and shake well. Makes ½ cup.

Stir together the peppery barbecue sauce for these ribs a day before barbecuing

so the flavors have time to blend.

BABY BACK PORK RIBS
(Pictured on pages 116–117)

1 recipe Busterback's Barbecue Sauce
4 to 6 pounds pork baby loin back ribs
⅛ teaspoon salt
⅛ teaspoon pepper
⅛ teaspoon paprika

About 24 hours before cooking ribs, prepare sauce. ♦ Season ribs with salt, pepper, and paprika. To precook ribs before grilling or baking them, place the ribs, meaty sides up, on a rack in a shallow roasting pan. Tightly cover with foil. Bake ribs in a 350° oven for 1 hour. If desired, refrigerate the precooked ribs until time to grill or bake them. ♦ *To grill ribs,* in a covered grill arrange *medium-hot* coals around a foil drip pan. Test for *medium* heat by placing your hand above the pan. You should be able to hold your hand there for 4 seconds. Place ribs, meaty sides up, on the grill rack over the drip pan but not over the coals. Lower grill hood. Grill about 30 minutes (allow up to 45 minutes, if ribs were chilled) or till ribs are tender, brushing occasionally with some of the sauce during last 15 minutes of grilling. ♦ Or, *to bake ribs,* drain fat from ribs in roasting pan. Continue baking ribs, uncovered, for 30 to 45 minutes more or till tender, brushing occasionally with sauce. ♦ To serve, heat and pass remaining sauce with ribs. Makes 6 to 8 servings.
♦ **Busterback's Barbecue Sauce:** In a covered container stir together 1 cup *catsup;* ¼ cup packed *brown sugar;* ¼ cup prepared *mustard;* 2 tablespoons chopped *onion;* 1 tablespoon *vinegar;* 1 to 2 teaspoons *pepper;* 1 clove *garlic,* minced; and ¼ teaspoon *liquid smoke.* Cover and refrigerate about 24 hours to allow flavors to blend. Makes 1½ cups.

Busterback's mouth-watering barbecued steaks are irresistible. They're marinated

for extra flavor, then brushed with molasses to add a hint of sweetness.

BARBECUED STEAKS
(Pictured on pages 116–117)

3 pounds beef top loin *or* rib eye steaks, cut ¾ inch thick
1 large onion, sliced
⅓ cup snipped parsley
3 shallots, thinly sliced
3 bay leaves
3 teaspoons whole black peppers, crushed
⅛ teaspoon crushed red pepper
1¼ cups dry red wine
Salt
Pepper
2 tablespoons molasses

Place steaks in a plastic bag set in a large bowl. Add sliced onion, parsley, shallots, bay leaves, crushed black peppers, and red pepper. Then pour wine into bag. Close bag and marinate steaks in the refrigerator for 2 to 4 hours, turning the bag occasionally. ♦ Remove the steaks from the bag and reserve the marinade. ♦ *To grill steaks,* in an uncovered grill spread coals out in a single layer. Test for *medium-hot* heat by placing your hand above the coals. You should be able to hold your hand there for 3 seconds. Place steaks on the grill rack. Season with salt and pepper. Grill to desired doneness, turning once and brushing occasionally with the reserved marinade. (Allow 8 to 9 minutes total for rare, 10 to 12 minutes for medium, and 12 to 15 minutes for well-done.) During the last 5 minutes of grilling, brush both sides of the steaks with molasses. ♦ Or, *to broil steaks,* place steaks on the unheated rack of a broiler pan. Broil 4 to 5 inches from the heat to desired doneness, turning once and brushing occasionally with the reserved marinade. (Allow 8 to 9 minutes total for rare, 10 to 12 minutes for medium, and 12 to 15 minutes for well-done.) During the last 5 minutes of broiling, brush both sides of steaks with molasses. Makes 6 to 8 servings.

These light, airy buttermilk biscuits take their name from the majestic

Sawtooth Mountains, which are nearby.

SAWTOOTH BISCUITS

2 cups all-purpose flour
1 tablespoon baking powder
½ teaspoon salt
½ cup shortening
¾ cup buttermilk

In a medium mixing bowl stir together flour, baking powder, and salt. Cut in shortening till mixture resembles coarse crumbs. Make a well in center of the dry mixture, then add buttermilk all at once. Use a fork to stir just till moistened. ♦ Turn the dough out onto a lightly floured surface. Quickly knead the dough by gently folding and pressing the dough for 10 to 12 strokes or till the dough is *nearly* smooth. ♦ Lightly roll dough to about ¼-inch thickness. Cut dough with a floured 2½-inch biscuit cutter, dipping the cutter into flour between cuts. ♦ Place biscuits on an ungreased baking sheet. Bake in a 325° oven for 18 to 20 minutes or till golden. Makes 24.

On the trail, Kevin cooks these potatoes in a Dutch oven over a campfire. For

home convenience, this recipe was converted for use on a range top or grill.

CHEESY POTATOES
(Pictured on pages 116–117)

2 tablespoons cooking oil
2 pounds potatoes, thinly sliced (6 cups)
2 small cloves garlic, minced
½ teaspoon salt
⅛ teaspoon pepper
1 large onion, chopped (1 cup)
⅓ cup chopped sweet red pepper
⅓ cup chopped sweet green pepper
1 cup shredded cheddar cheese (4 ounces)

In a heavy 12-inch skillet on the range top, heat oil over medium-low heat. Add potatoes, garlic, salt, and pepper. Cover and cook for 10 minutes, stirring occasionally. ◆ Stir onion and red and green peppers into potatoes in skillet. Cover and cook for 20 to 25 minutes more or till potatoes are tender, stirring occasionally. ◆ Sprinkle cheese over potatoes. Remove skillet from heat and let stand, covered, for 2 to 3 minutes or till cheese is melted. Makes 6 to 8 servings.
◆ **Grill method:** Tear off two 36x14-inch pieces of *heavy* foil. Fold foil in half to make two 14-inch rectangles. Fold up sides, forming 2 pouches. Divide potatoes between pouches. Drizzle potatoes with the oil; sprinkle with garlic, salt, and pepper. Layer onion and red and green peppers on top of the potatoes. Fold edges of foil together to seal pouches securely, leaving space for steam to expand. ◆ In a covered or an uncovered grill, test for *medium-hot* coals by placing your hand above the coals. You should be able to hold your hand there for 3 seconds. Place the pouches on the grill rack over the coals and grill for 25 to 30 minutes or till potatoes are tender (turn pouches over occasionally if using an uncovered grill). ◆ Carefully open pouches. Sprinkle cheese over potatoes. Close the pouches and let the potatoes stand for 3 to 4 minutes or till cheese is melted.

Take a cue from Kevin's trail-ride menu. Apple crisp is the perfect no-fuss dessert—

it uses just a few ingredients, goes together in no time, and tastes great.

APPLE CRISP

1 cup sugar
¾ cup all-purpose flour
½ cup butter *or* margarine
8 medium baking apples, peeled, cored, and sliced (8 cups)
2 teaspoons ground cinnamon
1 teaspoon ground nutmeg
2 teaspoons lemon juice
¼ cup water

For topping, in a medium mixing bowl stir together sugar and flour. Cut in butter or margarine till mixture resembles coarse crumbs. Set topping aside. ♦ For filling, in a large mixing bowl place apples. Sprinkle with cinnamon and nutmeg. Toss, then sprinkle with lemon juice and toss again till apples are coated. ♦ Transfer filling to an ungreased 8x8x2-inch baking dish. Drizzle water over apples, then sprinkle with topping. Bake in a 375° oven about 30 minutes or till apples are tender. Makes 6 to 8 servings.

*Harbor House—Inn by the Sea
in Elk, California*

Dinner
by
the Sea

If it's a peaceful,
leisurely meal in a spectacular setting that
guests want, they can't miss with
Harbor House, located on a 140-foot-high
cliff overlooking the Pacific Ocean.

MENU

Tomato-Basil Soup (page 131) ♦ *Pepper-Cheese Bread (page 132)*

Mixed Salad Greens with Lemon-Chive Vinaigrette (page 133)

Salmon Fillets in Phyllo (page 134) or *Mesquite-Grilled Salmon Steaks*

Fresh Asparagus Spears

Great Aunt Bess' Lemon Pudding Cake (page 135)

Iced Water ♦ *Freshly Brewed Coffee*

Where schooners once anchored on northern Calfornia's Mendocino coast, stands a sturdy, redwood inn called Harbor House. Here overnight and dinner guests are treated to a culinary voyage while enjoying the breathtaking setting atop a coastal bluff.

The fare at Harbor House features flavor combinations from around the globe. Many of the ingredients, however, are from the inn's own gardens.

Helen Turner, who owns Harbor House with her husband, Dean, is especially proud of the inn's herb and vegetable gardens. The gardens not only provide produce for the table, but also act as functional landscaping.

It was this combination of spectacular location and lovely gardens that drew Helen and Dean to Harbor House. They had been running another inn, but made the switch when Harbor House came up for sale. "At Harbor House, we found a way to continue our interest in entertaining, wholesome food, beauty, clean air, and living by the sea," says Helen.

"At Harbor House, we found a way to continue our interest in entertaining, wholesome food, beauty, clean air, and living by the sea."

A typical dinner at Harbor House begins with homemade Tomato-Basil Soup,

Pepper-Cheese Bread, and a salad of mixed greens.

TOMATO-BASIL SOUP
(Pictured on pages 128–129)

2½ **pounds tomatoes, peeled, seeded, and cut up, (about 6 cups)**
or **two 16-ounce cans tomatoes**
¼ **cup lightly packed fresh basil leaves**
or **1 tablespoon dried basil, crushed**
1 cup chicken broth
1 tablespoon sugar
Dash to ¼ teaspoon salt
Dash ground red pepper
Dash ground black pepper
Dash bottled hot pepper sauce
Desired fresh herb (optional)

In a blender container or food processor bowl place about *half* of the fresh or *undrained* canned tomatoes and all of the basil. Cover and blend or process till smooth. Transfer pureed tomato mixture to a medium saucepan. Repeat blending or processing with remaining tomatoes. ◆ Stir chicken broth, sugar, salt, red and black pepper, and hot pepper sauce into the tomato mixture. Bring to boiling, then reduce heat. Cover and simmer for 30 minutes. ◆ Serve immediately. *Or,* transfer to a covered container and refrigerate. To serve, ladle warm or chilled soup into small bowls. If desired, garnish each serving with a fresh herb. Makes 6 (¾-cup) servings.

PEPPER-CHEESE BREAD

(Pictured on pages 128–129)

¼ cup *warm* water (105° to 115°)
1 package active dry yeast
½ teaspoon sugar
⅛ teaspoon ground ginger
5½ to 6 cups all-purpose flour
⅓ cup nonfat dry milk powder
2 tablespoons sugar
1 to 1½ teaspoons pepper
2 cups shredded cheddar cheese (8 ounces)
1½ cups *very warm* water (120° to 130°)
2 tablespoons cooking oil
1 slightly beaten egg
1 slightly beaten egg yolk

In a small bowl combine ¼ cup warm water, dry yeast, ½ teaspoon sugar, and ginger; let stand 5 minutes or till bubbles form. ♦ In a large bowl stir together *1½ cups* of the flour, milk powder, 2 tablespoons sugar, pepper, and 1 teaspoon *salt.* ♦ Stir yeast mixture, cheese, 1½ cups very warm water, oil, and whole egg into flour mixture. Beat with an electric mixer on low speed 30 seconds. Beat on high speed 3 minutes. Using a spoon, stir in as much of the remaining flour as you can. ♦ Turn dough out onto a lightly floured surface. Knead in enough of the remaining flour to make a moderately stiff dough that is smooth and elastic (6 to 8 minutes). Shape dough into a ball; place in a greased bowl, and turn once to grease surface. Cover; let rise in a warm place till double in size (about 1 hour). ♦ Punch dough down; turn out onto a floured surface. Cover; let rest 10 minutes. ♦ Meanwhile, grease 2 baking sheets. ♦ Divide dough in half. Divide *each* half into *three* equal portions. ♦ To shape loaves, roll each portion into a 16-inch-long rope. Braid by lining up *three* ropes, 1 inch apart on a prepared baking sheet. Starting in middle, *loosely* braid by bringing left rope underneath the center rope; bring right rope under new center rope. Repeat to end. On the other end, braid by bringing outside ropes alternately *over* center rope. Press ends together to seal. Repeat shaping remaining 3 ropes on second baking sheet. Cover; let rise in a warm place till *nearly* double (about 30 minutes). ♦ Brush loaves with a mixture of egg yolk and 1 tablespoon *water.* Bake in a 350° oven 20 minutes or till golden and bread sounds hollow when tapped. Makes 2 loaves.

Helen suggests using extra-virgin olive oil and freshly ground black pepper in this

flavorful vinaigrette.

LEMON-CHIVE VINAIGRETTE
(Pictured on pages 128–129)

½ **cup olive oil**
¼ **cup lemon juice**
3 tablespoons finely snipped chives
or **finely chopped green onion tops**
1 to 2 tablespoons honey*
1 tablespoon snipped fresh basil *or* **1 teaspoon dried basil, crushed**
1 tablespoon red wine vinegar
Dash salt
Dash pepper

In a screw-top jar combine olive oil, lemon juice, chives or green onion tops, honey, basil, red wine vinegar, salt, and pepper. Cover and shake well. Let vinaigrette stand for 30 minutes to 1 hour so flavors can blend. Shake before serving. ♦ If desired, store vinaigrette in the refrigerator for up to 2 weeks. Bring vinaigrette back to room temperature before using. Makes 1 cup.
♦ *If salad greens are quite tart, you may need to adjust the sweetness of this tangy vinaigrette by adding more than the 2 tablespoons honey.
♦ **Note:** At Harbor House, Helen uses this vinaigrette on a mixture of tender salad greens such as Bibb lettuce, leaf lettuce, arugula, and kale, and edible flowers such as marigolds, violas, pansies, nasturtiums, and rose petals.

SALMON FILLETS IN PHYLLO

2¼ **pounds skinless salmon fillets**
¼ **cup butter** *or* **margarine**
¼ **cup all-purpose flour**
1 **cup fish stock** *or* **bottled clam juice**
1 **cup milk, light cream,** *or* **half-and-half**
2 **tablespoons grated Parmesan cheese**
½ **teaspoon white pepper**
¼ **teaspoon ground cumin**
Dash bottled hot pepper sauce
18 **18x12-inch sheets frozen phyllo**
dough, thawed (about 12 ounces)
¾ **cup butter** *or* **margarine, melted**
Fresh dill *or* **edible flowers (optional)**

Cut salmon fillets into six 6-ounce portions; set aside. ♦ For sauce, in a saucepan melt the ¼ cup butter or margarine. Stir in flour. Then stir in fish stock and milk. Cook and stir till thickened and bubbly. Stir in Parmesan cheese, white pepper, cumin, and hot pepper sauce; set aside. ♦ To assemble bundles, unfold phyllo. Place 1 sheet of phyllo on a waxed-paper-lined cutting board; brush with some of the ¾ cup melted butter or margarine. Top with a second sheet of phyllo; brush with more butter and top with a third sheet of phyllo. (Cover remaining phyllo with a damp towel to prevent drying out; set aside.) Place a portion of salmon diagonally across and near the end of one corner of the phyllo stack. Spoon *2 tablespoons* of sauce on top. Fold bottom corner of phyllo up and over sauce and fillet; fold in side corners. Continue folding phyllo from bottom to form a bundle. ♦ Repeat making bundles with remaining phyllo dough, melted butter or margarine, salmon, and sauce. Set remaining melted butter and sauce aside. ♦ Butter a 15x10x1-inch baking pan. Place bundles in pan. Brush tops of bundles with remaining melted butter. Bake in a 400° oven about 20 minutes or till golden. ♦ To serve, heat the reserved sauce over low heat just till heated through. Spoon sauce over the top of each bundle. If desired, garnish with dill or edible flowers. Serves 6. ♦ **Note:** To make ahead, prepare and assemble bundles as above. Place bundles on the buttered baking sheet. Brush with the remaining melted butter, but *do not bake.* Cover and refrigerate for up to 4 hours. Cover and refrigerate remaining sauce. ♦ To serve, uncover and bake bundles in a 400° oven about 25 minutes or till golden. Heat remaining sauce to serve over bundles and garnish as above.

Many recipes at Harbor House are longtime favorites. This dessert was handed

down by Helen's Great Aunt Bess.

GREAT AUNT BESS' LEMON PUDDING CAKE

¾ **cup sugar**
¼ **cup all-purpose flour**
⅛ **teaspoon salt**
4 **teaspoons finely shredded lemon peel**
⅓ **cup lemon juice**
2 **tablespoons butter** *or* **margarine, melted**
3 **slightly beaten egg yolks**
1½ **cups milk**
3 **egg whites**
½ **cup whipping cream, whipped (optional)**
Desired berries (optional)

Grease a 1½-quart soufflé dish or casserole; set aside. ♦ In a large mixing bowl stir together sugar, flour, and salt. Then stir in lemon peel, lemon juice, and melted butter or margarine. ♦ Stir together egg yolks and milk; add to the flour mixture. Stir just till mixture is combined. ♦ In a medium mixing bowl beat egg whites with an electric mixer on medium to high speed just till stiff peaks form (tips stand straight). Gently fold egg whites into lemon mixture. Spoon batter into the prepared soufflé dish or casserole. ♦ Place the soufflé dish or casserole in a shallow baking pan, then set the baking pan on the oven rack. Pour *boiling* or *hottest tap water* into the shallow baking pan to a depth of 1 inch. Bake in a 350° oven for 35 to 40 minutes or till the top is lightly browned. ♦ Serve warm. If desired, serve with whipped cream and berries. Makes 8 servings.

NUTRITION INFORMATION

Page	Recipe	Servings	Calories	Protein (g)	Carbo-hydrates (g)	Total Fat (g)	Saturated Fat (g)	Choles-terol (mg)	Sodium (mg)
112	Amaretto Cheesecake	12	704	14	47	52	24	171	341
53	Apple Cider Syrup	6	123	0	23	4	2	10	34
127	Apple Crisp	6	432	2	74	16	10	41	132
76	Apple 'n' Juice Sorbet	24	59	0	15	0	0	0	1
10	Apple Soup	8	205	2	35	6	3	17	21
104	Apricot-Amaretto Surprise Ice Cream	18	548	4	32	46	27	240	45
38	Apricot-Cheese Coffee Cake	9	387	9	50	17	6	67	612
123	Baby Back Pork Ribs	6	290	31	22	10	4	83	711
30	Bacon-Cheddar Muffins	8	281	8	29	15	4	40	212
18	Bacon 'n' Wild Rice Egg Casseroles	5	643	26	16	53	27	516	584
59	Baked Apples in Brandy Sauce	8	236	0	54	0	0	0	14
27	Baked Pecan French Toast	4	790	13	73	52	25	308	566
26	Baked Victorian French Toast	4	609	14	84	25	13	316	484
20	Banana Pecan Pancakes	4	619	12	115	14	5	72	267
124	Barbecued Steaks	6	410	49	8	15	6	130	298
90	Beef Fillets with Red Chili Sauce	4	489	39	5	34	19	190	605
86	Blinden Vinken	4	442	48	10	23	9	268	743
11	Blintz Soufflé	6	422	11	42	24	14	196	347
45	Blueberry Lemon Bread	16	153	3	24	5	3	39	138
98	Boneless Breast of Country Chicken	4	300	29	11	15	5	87	374
115	Bread Pudding Supreme	8	746	13	100	33	19	219	568
65	Caviar Pie	14	152	6	2	14	6	155	195
126	Cheesy Potatoes	6	290	9	40	11	5	20	308
96	Chicken Florentine	4	497	52	23	23	9	139	1124
104	Chocolate Ice Cream	18	515	4	31	43	26	240	45
32	Chocolate-Orange Muffins	18	188	3	26	9	5	40	106
39	Churros	10	252	4	29	14	5	102	105
24	Cornmeal Waffles	8	288	6	30	16	3	32	281
16	Country Salmon Pie	6	762	32	31	57	33	322	724
80	Crab Fondue	6	428	13	23	33	6	45	617
97	Crab 'n' Cilantro Stuffed Chicken Breasts	4	454	40	11	28	8	120	532
81	Cranberry Consommé	8	107	1	24	0	0	0	8
83	Cream of Fennel Soup	4	249	4	8	22	14	61	316
74	Eat-Me Cakes	24	66	1	6	4	3	28	39
58	English Country Wassail	21	245	1	59	0	0	0	12
110	English Red Raspberry Trifle	8	783	9	83	48	16	223	369
25	Fancy Stuffed French Toast	8	488	13	67	19	10	175	499
33	French Apple-Butter Muffins	12	214	3	28	10	6	45	105
102	Fresh Broccoli Slaw	6	126	2	10	10	1	5	242
7	"Fuzzy" Fruit Juice Cocktails	5	62	0	15	0	0	0	1
122	Gazpacho Salad	6	244	8	8	21	7	25	248
22	Gingerbread Pancakes	5	416	7	63	15	5	61	291
135	Great Aunt Bess' Lemon Pudding Cake	8	166	4	25	6	3	92	104
92	Grilled Lamb with Honey-Mustard Sauce	8	556	26	12	45	25	197	414
12	Hachland Hill's Egg Soufflé	6	439	17	10	36	15	340	567
23	Heavenly Hots	4	354	7	51	15	8	132	316
101	Homemade Hirtensilat	4	170	3	7	16	6	23	277
19	Honeymooners' Casseroles	2	676	36	37	44	22	305	836
108	Hot Walnut Fudge Cake à la Mode	24	423	6	57	20	11	80	141

Page	Recipe	Servings	Per Serving						
			Calories	Protein (g)	Carbo-hydrates (g)	Total Fat (g)	Saturated Fat (g)	Choles-terol (mg)	Sodium (mg)
40	Kringler	16	205	3	18	13	8	73	115
57	Lemonade	12	136	0	36	0	0	0	1
133	Lemon-Chive Vinaigrette	16	65	0	2	7	1	0	8
114	Lemon Imperial	8	385	5	43	23	12	107	156
85	Lobster 'n' Wild Rice Salad	4	532	20	34	37	3	41	296
61	Maple and Pecan Cookies	36	147	2	11	11	4	20	44
96	Marinara Sauce	10	55	1	7	3	0	0	315
89	Marinated Beef Tenderloin	4	305	36	1	15	5	108	372
75	Meringue Mushrooms	40	27	0	6	0	0	0	6
55	Orange Muffins	18	197	3	34	6	4	39	137
31	Peach Delight Bran Muffins	18	141	3	27	4	1	12	163
41	Pecan Horns	36	167	2	16	12	6	24	73
121	Peel-and-Eat Shrimp	6	83	10	9	0	0	83	560
132	Pepper-Cheese Bread	64	63	2	9	2	1	11	25
35	Peppertrees' Chocolate Coffee Cake	16	316	4	42	16	8	51	145
34	Peppertrees' Coffee Coffee Cake	16	318	4	43	15	8	51	144
107	Poached Pears with Grand Marnier Sauce	4	502	3	92	14	8	147	18
29	Popovers Romanoff	6	317	8	33	17	10	105	180
95	Pork Tenderloin with Maple-Mustard Sauce	4	241	20	21	12	2	50	412
94	Pork Tenderloin with Plum Sauce	2	305	37	16	7	2	101	223
14	Puffy Crab Omelet	8	488	16	14	41	24	305	449
103	Pureed Sweet Potatoes	6	184	2	21	11	7	31	182
62	Quickie Quiches	12	165	6	11	11	4	66	124
54	Refrigerated Bran Muffins	24	197	4	37	5	1	19	278
47	Ricotta Cheese Pies	12	337	9	21	25	15	126	174
82	Roquefort-Vegetable Soup	6	264	6	7	25	15	80	589
134	Salmon Fillets in Phyllo	6	749	41	44	45	22	187	754
17	Sausage Strata	6	390	23	14	27	13	179	855
125	Sawtooth Biscuits	24	79	1	8	4	1	0	89
72	Scones	8	270	4	28	16	10	43	277
63	Seeded Sage 'n' Cheddar Wafers	96	27	1	2	2	1	5	23
64	Sharp Pineapple Spread	4	87	2	4	7	5	23	64
51	Skiers' Sausage	6	246	8	28	12	4	32	581
79	Steamed Penn Cove Mussels	3	300	6	2	26	16	79	138
46	Strawberries with Crème Fraîche	6	174	2	17	12	7	36	23
77	Strawberry Roulade	10	171	3	36	2	1	85	26
52	Stuffed French Toast Strata	6	757	22	77	40	22	376	815
105	Summer Fruits with Devonshire Cream	4	358	4	43	18	11	93	53
8	Swirled Melon Soup	6	77	1	18	0	0	0	16
88	Teng Dah Fillet	6	349	44	9	14	6	128	1471
109	Toasted Almond Torte	12	662	10	52	47	23	255	75
131	Tomato-Basil Soup	6	53	3	11	1	0	0	168
73	Treacle Tartlets	14	210	3	18	14	9	81	153
99	Tuna with Red Pepper Coulis	4	434	53	4	22	4	0	279
71	Turkey Tea Sandwiches	8	228	15	15	13	2	38	192
37	Walton's Mountain Coffee Cake	12	361	7	58	12	5	21	526

We analyzed the nutrition content of each recipe using the first ingredient if choices are given, and the first serving size if a serving range is given. We omitted optional ingredients from the analyses.

INDEX OF INNS

To help you in your travels, we're providing this list of the country inns and bed-and-breakfasts featured in our book. The listings were up-to-date at the time of publishing, but be sure to contact these establishments before visiting them to confirm the information.

Alaska

Glacier Bay Country Inn
Al and Annie Unrein, Innkeepers
P.O. Box 5–BHG
Gustavus, AK 99826
(907/697-2288)
♦ Recipe: Puffy Crab Omelet, 14

Arizona

Garland's Oak Creek Lodge
Gary and Mary Garland, Innkeepers
Highway 89–A
P.O. Box 152
Sedona, AZ 86336
(602/282-3343)
♦ Recipe: Beef Fillets with Red Chili Sauce, 90

Peppertrees Bed & Breakfast Inn
Marjorie G. Martin, Innkeeper
724 E. University Blvd.
Tucson, AZ 85719
(602/622-7167)
♦ Recipes: Maple and Pecan Cookies, 61; Peppertrees' Chocolate Coffee Cake, 35; Peppertrees' Coffee Coffee Cake, 34

California

Harbor House—Inn by the Sea
Helen and Dean Turner, Innkeepers
5600 S. Highway 1
P.O. Box 369
Elk, CA 95432
(707/877-3203)
♦ Recipes: Great Aunt Bess' Lemon Pudding Cake, 135; Lemon-Chive Vinaigrette, 133; Pepper-Cheese Bread, 132; Salmon Fillets in Phyllo, 134; Tomato-Basil Soup, 131

Hotel Carter
Mark and Christi Carter, Innkeepers
301 L St.
Eureka, CA 95501
(707/444-8062)
♦ Recipes: Grilled Lamb with Honey-Mustard Sauce, 92; Toasted Almond Torte, 109

Madrona Manor
John and Carol Muir, Innkeepers
1001 Westside Rd.
Healdsburg, CA 95448
(707/433-4231 or 707/433-4433)
♦ Recipe: Churros, 39

Colorado

San Juan Guest Ranch
Scott and Pat MacTiernan, Innkeepers
2882 County Rd. 2
Ridgway, CO 81432
(800-331-3015)
♦ Recipe: Homemade Hirtensilat, 101

Delaware

The David Finney Inn
Judy Piser, Innkeeper
216 Delaware St.
New Castle, DE 19720
(800-334-6640)
♦ Recipe: Pork Tenderloin with Plum Sauce, 94

Florida

The Fortnightly Inn
Frank and Judi Daley, Innkeepers
377 E. Fairbanks Ave.
Winter Park, FL 32789
(407/645-4440)
♦ Recipe: Peach Delight Bran Muffins, 31

Georgia

The Gastonian
Hugh and Roberta Lineberger, Innkeepers
220 E. Gaston St.
Savannah, GA 31401
(912/232-2869)
♦ Recipe: Sausage Strata, 17

Idaho

Busterback Ranch
Kevin G. O'Donnell, Innkeeper
Star Route
Ketchum, ID 83340
(208/774-2271)
♦ Recipes: Apple Crisp, 127; Baby Back Pork Ribs, 123; Barbecued Steaks, 124; Cheesy Potatoes, 126; Gazpacho Salad, 122; Peel-and-Eat Shrimp, 121; Sawtooth Biscuits, 125

Illinois

The Westerfield House, Inc.
Jim and Marilyn Westerfield, Innkeepers
R.R. 2, Box 34
Freeburg, IL 62243
(618/539-5643)
♦ Recipes: Lemonade, 57; Seeded Sage 'n' Cheddar Wafers, 63

Iowa

Hannah Marie Country Inn
Mary Nichols, Innkeeper
R.R. 1, Highway 71 S
Spencer, IA 51301
(712/262-1286)
♦ Recipes: Apple 'n' Juice Sorbet, 76; Eat-Me Cakes, 74; Meringue Mushrooms, 75; Scones, 72; Strawberry Roulade, 77; Treacle Tartlets, 73; Turkey Tea Sandwiches, 71

Spring Side Inn
Mark and Nancy Jaspers, Innkeepers
P.O. Box 41
Bellevue, IA 52031
(319/872-5452)
♦ Recipes: Gingerbread Pancakes, 22; Poached Pears with Grand Marnier Sauce, 107

Strawtown Inn
Roger Olson, General Manager
1111 Washington St.
Pella, IA 50219
(515/628-4043)
♦ Recipe: Blinden Vinken, 86

Kansas

Heritage House Historic Inn
Marilyn Kappler, General Manager
3535 SW. Sixth Ave.
Topeka, KS 66606
(913/233-3800)
♦ Recipe: Amaretto Cheesecake, 112

Swedish Country Inn
Virginia Brunsell, Innkeeper
112 W. Lincoln
Lindsborg, KS 67456
(913/227-2985)
♦ Recipe: Kringler, 40

Louisiana

Madewood
Keith and Millie Marshall, Innkeepers
4250 Highway 308
Napoleonville, LA 70390
(504/369-7151)
♦ Recipe: Bread Pudding Supreme, 115

Maine

The Blue Hill Inn
Mary and Don Hartley, Innkeepers
Union Street
P.O. Box 403
Blue Hill, ME 04614
(207/374-2844)
♦ Recipe: Lobster 'n' Wild Rice Salad, 85

The Newcastle Inn
Chris and Ted Sprague, Innkeepers
River Road
R.R. 2, Box 24
Newcastle, ME 04533
(207/563-5685 or 800-832-8669)
♦ Recipes: Blueberry Lemon Bread, 45; Ricotta Cheese Pies, 47; Strawberries with Crème Fraîche, 46

Penobscot Meadows Inn
Dini and Bernie Chapnick, Innkeepers

R.R. 1
Belfast, ME 04915-1298
(207/338-5320)
♦ Recipe: Penobscot Meadows' Homemade Ice Creams (Apricot-Amaretto Surprise Ice Cream; Chocolate Ice Cream), 104

Michigan

The Inn at Union Pier
Madeleine and Bill Reinke and Libby Johnston, Innkeepers
9708 Berrien St.
P.O. Box 222
Union Pier, MI 49129
(616/469-4700)
♦ Recipes: Blintz Soufflé, 11; Popovers Romanoff, 29

The Victorian Villa Inn
Ronald J. and Susan L. Gibson, Innkeepers
601 N. Broadway St.
Union City, MI 49094
(517/741-7383)
♦ Recipes: Baked Apples in Brandy Sauce, 59; English Country Wassail, 58; English Red Raspberry Trifle, 110

Minnesota

The Asa Parker House
Marjorie Bush, Innkeeper
17500 St. Croix Trail N
Marine on the St. Croix, MN 55047
(612/433-5248)
♦ Recipe: Bacon 'n' Wild Rice Egg Casseroles, 18

Park Row Bed & Breakfast
Ann L. Burckhardt, Innkeeper
525 W. Park Row
St. Peter, MN 56082
(507/931-2495)
♦ Recipes: "Fuzzy" Fruit Juice Cocktails, 7; Honeymooners' Casseroles, 19

Mississippi

Millsaps Buie House
Judy Fenter, Dottie Stewart, and Nancy Fleming, Innkeepers
628 N. State St.
Jackson, MS 39202
(601/352-0221)
♦ Recipe: Pecan Horns, 41

Monmouth Plantation
Bob Kenna, Manager; Ron and Lani Riches, Innkeepers
36 Melrose Ave. at the John A. Quitman Pkwy.
Natchez, MS 39120
(601/442-5852)
♦ Recipe: Caviar Pie, 65

Missouri

The Andrew King House
Jim and Rosemary Wessely, Innkeepers
305 Glyn Cagny Rd.
Ballwin, MO 63021
(314/394-1925)
♦ Recipe: Swirled Melon Soup, 8

Montana

Lone Mountain Ranch
Bob and Vivian Schaap and Mike Ankeny, Innkeepers
P.O. Box 69
Big Sky, MT 59716
(406/995-4644)
♦ Recipes: Crab 'n' Cilantro Stuffed Chicken Breasts, 97; Heavenly Hots, 23

New Jersey

Barnard-Good House
Nan and Tom Hawkins, Innkeepers
28 Perry St.
Cape May, NJ 08204
(609/884-5381)
♦ Recipes: Apple Soup, 10

New Mexico

Grant Corner Inn
Louise S. Stewart and Martin (Pat) S. Walter, Innkeepers
122 Grant Ave.
Santa Fe, NM 87501
(505/983-6678)
♦ Recipes: Chocolate-Orange Muffins, 32; French Apple-Butter Muffins, 33

New York

Sarah's Dream
Judi Williams and Ken Morusty, Innkeepers
49 W. Main St.
P.O. Box 1087
Dryden, NY 13053
(607/844-4321)
♦ Recipe: Quickie Quiches, 62

North Carolina

Colonel Ludlow Inn
Ken Land, Innkeeper
Summit and West Fifth
Winston-Salem, NC 27101
(919/777-1887)
♦ Recipe: Bacon-Cheddar Muffins, 30

Mast Farm Inn
Sibyl and Francis Pressly, Innkeepers
P.O. Box 704
Valle Crucis, NC 28691
(704/963-5857)
♦ Recipe: Apricot-Cheese Coffee Cake, 38

The Oakwood Inn
Terri Jones, Innkeeper
411 N. Bloodworth St.
Raleigh, NC 27604
(919/832-9712)
♦ Recipe: Baked Pecan French Toast, 27

Ohio

Buxton Inn—1812
Orville and Audrey Orr,
    Innkeepers
313 E. Broadway
Granville, OH 43023
(614/587-0001)
◆ Recipe: Hot Walnut
Fudge Cake à la
Mode, 108

The Inn at Cedar Falls
Anne Castle, Ellen
    Grinsfelder, Karen
    Nesbitt, and Debra
    Coyan, Innkeepers
21190 State Route 374
Logan, OH 43138
(614/385-7489)
◆ Recipe: Fancy Stuffed
French Toast, 25

The Inn at Honey Run
Marjorie Stock,
    Innkeeper
6920 Country Rd. 203
Millersburg, OH 44654
(216/674-0011)
◆ Recipes: Boneless
Breast of Country
Chicken, 98; Fresh
Broccoli Slaw, 102

Oregon

**The Winchester
    Country Inn**
Michael and Laurie
    Gibbs, Innkeepers
35 S. Second St.
Ashland, OR 97520
(503/488-1113)
◆ Recipes: Crab Fondue,
80; Teng Dah Fillet, 88

Pennsylvania

Eagles Mere Inn
Lou and Joan Fiocchi,
    Innkeepers
Mary Avenue
P.O. Box 356
Eagles Mere, PA 17731
(717/525-3273)
◆ Recipes: Roquefort-
Vegetable Soup, 82;
Sharp Pineapple
Spread, 64

The Inn at Phillips Mill
Brooks and Joyce
    Kaufman, Innkeepers
North River Road
New Hope, PA 18938
(215/862-2984)
◆ Recipe: Pureed Sweet
Potatoes, 103

Rhode Island

Hotel Manisses
Joan and Justin Abrams,
    Innkeepers
Spring Street
Block Island, RI 02807
(401/466-2063)
◆ Recipe: Tuna with Red
Pepper Coulis, 99

South Carolina

Liberty Hall Inn
Tom and Susan Jonas,
    Innkeepers
Business Highway 28
Pendleton, SC 29670
(803/646-7500)
◆ Recipes: Chicken
Florentine, 96; Marinara
Sauce, 96; Marinated
Beef Tenderloin, 89

Villa de La Fontaine
William A. Fontaine,
    Innkeeper
138 Wentworth St.
Charleston, SC 29401
(803/577-7709)
◆ Recipe: Cornmeal
Waffles, 24

Tennessee

Hachland Hill
Phila Hach and Joe
    Hach, Innkeepers
1601 Madison St.
Clarksville, TN 37043
(615/647-4084)
◆ Recipe: Hachland
Hill's Egg Soufflé, 12

Texas

The Oxford House
Bill and Paula Oxford,
    Innkeepers
563 N. Graham
Stephenville, TX 76401
(817/965-6885)
◆ Recipe: Baked
Victorian French
Toast, 26

Utah

Washington School Inn
Nancy Beaufait, Manager;
    Delphine Covington,
    Cathy Elliott, and
    Karen Guthrie,
    Innkeepers
543 Park Ave.
P.O. Box 536
Park City, UT 84060
(801/649-3800)
◆ Recipes: Apple Cider
Syrup, 53; Orange
Muffins, 55; Refrigerated
Bran Muffins, 54; Skiers'
Sausage, 51; Stuffed
French Toast Strata, 52

Vermont

The Arlington Inn
Paul and Madeline
    Kruzel, Innkeepers
Historic Route 7A
Arlington, VT 05250
(802/375-6532)
◆ Recipe: Summer Fruits
with Devonshire
Cream, 105

Windham Hill Inn
Ken and Linda Busteed,
    Innkeepers
R.R. 1, Box 44
West Townshend, VT
05359
(802/874-4080)
◆ Recipes: Lemon
Imperial, 114; Pork
Tenderloin with Maple-
Mustard Sauce, 95

Virginia

The Norris House Inn
Amy Marasco, Innkeeper
108 Loudoun St. SW
Leesburg, VA 22075
(703/777-1806)
◆ Recipe: Walton's
Mountain Coffee
Cake, 37

Washington

**The Captain Whidbey
    Inn**
Capt. John Colby
    Stone, Innkeeper
2072 W. Captain
Whidbey Inn Rd.
Coupeville, WA 98239
(206/678-4097)
◆ Recipe: Steamed Penn
Cove Mussels, 79

**The Shelburne Country
    Inn**
Laurie Anderson and
    David Campiche,
    Innkeepers
P.O. Box 250
Seaview, WA 98644
(206/642-2442)
◆ Recipes: Banana Pecan
Pancakes, 20; Country
Salmon Pie, 16

West Virginia

Hillbrook Inn
Gretchen Carroll,
    Innkeeper
R.R. 2, Box 152
Charles Town, WV 25414
(304/725-4223)
◆ Recipe: Cream of
Fennel Soup, 83

Wisconsin

Old Rittenhouse Inn
Jerry and Mary Phillips,
    Innkeepers
P.O. Box 584
Bayfield, WI 54814
(715/779-5111)
◆ Recipe: Cranberry
Consommé, 81

INDEX OF RECIPES

Editor's Tips

METRIC COOKING HINTS

By making a few conversions, cooks in Australia, Canada, and the United Kingdom can use the recipes in Better Homes and Gardens® *Favorite Recipes from Country Inns and Bed-and-Breakfasts* with confidence. The charts on this page provide a guide for converting measurements from the U.S. customary system, which is used throughout this book, to the imperial and metric systems. There also is a conversion table for oven temperatures to accommodate the differences in oven calibrations.

♦ **Volume and Weight:** Americans traditionally use *cup* measures for liquid and solid ingredients. The chart at top right shows the approximate imperial and metric equivalents. If you are accustomed to weighing solid ingredients, here are some helpful approximate equivalents:
♦ 1 cup butter, caster sugar, or rice = 8 ounces = about 250 grams
♦ 1 cup flour = 4 ounces = about 125 grams
♦ 1 cup icing sugar = 5 ounces = about 150 grams
Spoon measures are used for smaller amounts of ingredients. Although the size of the teaspoon is the same, the size of the tablespoon varies slightly among countries. However, for practical purposes and for recipes in this book, a straight substitution is all that's necessary.

Measurements made using cups or spoons always should be *level*, unless stated otherwise.

♦ **Product Differences:** Most of the products and ingredients called for in the recipes in this book are available in English-speaking countries. However, some are known by different names. Here are some common American ingredients and their possible counterparts:
♦ Sugar is granulated or caster sugar.
♦ Powdered sugar is icing sugar.
♦ All-purpose flour is plain household flour or white flour. When self-rising flour is used in place of all-purpose flour in a recipe that calls for leavening, omit the leavening (baking soda or baking powder) and salt.
♦ Light corn syrup is golden syrup.
♦ Cornstarch is cornflour.
♦ Baking soda is bicarbonate of soda.
♦ Vanilla is vanilla essence.

♦ ♦ ♦

USEFUL EQUIVALENTS

¼ cup = 2 fluid ounces = 50ml
⅓ cup = 3 fluid ounces = 75ml
½ cup = 4 fluid ounces = 125ml
¾ cup = 6 fluid ounces = 175ml
1 cup = 8 fluid ounces = 250ml

⅛ teaspoon = 0.5ml	2 cups = 1 pint
¼ teaspoon = 1ml	1¾ pints = 1 litre
½ teaspoon = 2ml	½ inch = 1 centimetre
1 teaspoon = 5ml	1 inch = 2 centimetres

♦ ♦ ♦

BAKING PAN SIZES

American	Metric
8x1½-inch round baking pan	20x4-centimetre sandwich or cake tin
9x1½-inch round baking pan	23x3.5-centimetre sandwich or cake tin
11x7x1½-inch baking pan	28x18x4-centimetre baking pan
13x9x2-inch baking pan	32.5x23x5-centimetre baking pan
12x7½x2-inch baking dish	30x19x5-centimetre baking pan
15x10x2-inch baking pan	38x25.5x2.5-centimetre baking pan (Swiss roll tin)
9-inch pie plate	22x4- or 23x4-centimetre pie plate
7- or 8-inch springform pan	18- or 20-centimetre springform or loose-bottom cake tin
9x5x3-inch loaf pan	23x13x6-centimetre or 2-pound narrow loaf pan
1½-quart casserole	1.5-litre casserole
2-quart casserole	2-litre casserole

♦ ♦ ♦

OVEN TEMPERATURE EQUIVALENTS

Fahrenheit Setting	Celsius Setting*	Gas Setting
300°F	150°C	Gas Mark 2
325°F	160°C	Gas Mark 3
350°F	180°C	Gas Mark 4
375°F	190°C	Gas Mark 5
400°F	200°C	Gas Mark 6
425°F	220°C	Gas Mark 7
450°F	230°C	Gas Mark 8
Broil		Grill

*Electric and gas ovens may be calibrated using Celsius. However, increase the Celsius setting 10 to 20 degrees when cooking above 160°C with an *electric* oven. For *convection* or *forced-air* ovens (gas or electric), lower the temperature setting 10°C when cooking at all heat levels.